COMPROMISING
REDEMPTION

LITERARY
CURRENTS
IN
BIBLICAL
INTERPRETATION

EDITORS

Danna Nolan Fewell
Perkins School of Theology,
Southern Methodist University, Dallas TX
David M. Gunn
Columbia Theological Seminary, Decatur GA

EDITORIAL ADVISORY BOARD

COMPROMISING REDEMPTION

relating characters in the book of ruth

DANNA NOLAN FEWELL
&
DAVID MILLER GUNN

Westminster/John Knox Press
Louisville, Kentucky

COMPROMISING REDEMPTION:
RELATING CHARACTERS IN THE BOOK OF RUTH

First edition

Published by Westminster/John Knox Press
Louisville, Kentucky

PRINTED IN THE UNITED STATES OF AMERICA
2 4 6 8 9 7 5 3 1

Library of Congress Cataloging-in-Publication Data

Fewell, Danna Nolan.
  Compromising redemption : relating characters in the book of Ruth / Danna Nolan Fewell & David Miller Gunn. — 1st ed.
      p.   cm. — (Literary currents in biblical interpretation)
  Includes bibliographical references and indexes.
  ISBN 0-664-25135-8

  1. Bible.   O.T.   Ruth—Criticism, interpretation, etc. 2. Naomi (Biblical character) 3. Boaz (Biblical character) 4. Ruth (Biblical character) I. Gunn, David Miller. II. Title. III. Series.
BS1315.2.F48 1990
222'.3506—dc20   90-38426

To our mothers,
Doris Boney Nolan and Jean Miller Gunn,
our mothers-in-law,
Ann Lofton Fewell and Ethel Naylor Almond,
and certain other
women of great character
(נשי חיל)
in our lives,
Mary Robert Boney, Mitsi Erma Nolan Loyd,
Mina Gunn Meredith, Lenore Miller Newnham,
Ruth Fagan Shrimpton

'Whither thou goest,' she said
thinking: 'Gods but that's a hellhole
desert dry arsehole
no man's land but here would be
an aloneness too stark to suffer
there would be you.'
So she said, elaborating, 'Thy people
will be my people,' meaning
take me into your family
and added as an afterthought
because she knew it would please
her sometime mother-in-law
(does death sever such legal bonds?)
and thy god shall be my god'
thinking: 'Now what was he called?'

. . . . 'Listen,'
she said to Boaz. 'Your kinsman's
widow, she's been like a second
mother to me. I couldn't
just walk out and leave her.'
And he looking at her rich
pastures said: 'Fine, bring
the old lady if you want her.'
And Ruth said: 'I do, I do.'

— Maureen Duffy
   from "Mother and the Girl,"
   Collected Poems 1949-1984

CONTENTS

SERIES
PREFACE

New currents in biblical interpretation are emerging. Questions about origins—authors, intentions, settings—and stages of composition are giving way to questions about the literary qualities of the Bible, the play of its language, the coherence of its final form, and the relations between text and readers.

Such literary criticism is rapidly acquiring sophistication as it learns from major developments in secular critical theory, especially in understanding the instability of language and the key role of readers in the production of meaning. Biblical critics are being called to recognize that a plurality of readings is an inevitable and legitimate consequence of the interpretive process. By the same token, interpreters are being challenged to take responsibility for the theological, social, and ethical implications of their readings.

Biblical interpretation is changing on the practical as well as the theoretical level. More readers, both inside and outside the academic guild, are discovering that the Bible in literary perspective can powerfully engage people's lives. Communities of faith where the Bible is foundational may find that literary criticism can make the Scripture accessible in a way that historical criticism seems unable to do.

Within these changes lie exciting opportunities for all who seek contemporary meaning in the ancient texts. The goal of the series is to encourage such change and such search, to breach the confines of traditional biblical criticism, and to open channels for new currents of interpretation.

—THE EDITORS

PREFACE

Our book started life in classes we taught together at Columbia Theological Seminary between 1985 and 1987. It grew and was hugely nourished in subsequent classes offered by one or other of us (and occasionally both) at Perkins School of Theology, Columbia Seminary, various other schools and many churches in North America and even New Zealand and Australia. The insights and sensibilities of many people who shared their readings of Ruth are now indelibly part of our own experience of the biblical story and comprise many of the threads of the reading we present here. Those vital interchanges in so many different communities of readers have been a joy to us. They have reminded us, too, that interpretation thrives on dialogue and the tolerant recognition of differences—of times, places, people and perspectives.

Some other occasions have been important to the sustaining of our project. The academic community has been an important testing ground. We first shaped core elements of the book as papers to the Society of Biblical Literature, presenting them to meetings of the Southeast Region in 1986 and 1987 and again to colloquia at Emory and Yale Universities and to the Southwest Biblical Studies Seminar. Revised versions of these papers have appeared in *Journal for the Study of the Old Testament* (40 [1988] and 45 [1989]). Our work has met with varying and often strong responses, both approving and disapproving, both kinds gratifying, since they have confirmed to us that our reading does indeed touch some issues important to people's lives.

Our retelling of Ruth was presented as a dramatic reading to an audience for Women's Week at Perkins in 1989. The enthusiastic reception greatly encouraged us to think that other audiences might find our midrash helpful. Betsy Singleton we thank for the invitation, and our grateful appreciation goes to

Rebecca Gruber, Joan Eubank, John Ockels and Kathryn Taylor for so splendidly giving voice to our words.

Our thanks go to the Lilly Endowment, through the agency of Perkins School of Theology, for major support for one of us (Danna) and to Columbia Theological Seminary for a contribution (to David) to help with the final preparation of the manuscript. Co-operative writing at long distance can be costly and we have valued the backing of our schools.

Some particular sources of support have also been important to us. Burke Long, esteemed friend and friendly critic, urged us to explore a different format for presenting our reading—hence the retelling of Part I. Our endlessly patient spouses, David and Margaret, have rearranged their lives more times than we care to count in order to facilitate our writing together. Rebecca and Jonathan have watched their father board a plane for Dallas so often they think it is part of his normal routine. Danna's mother, Doris Nolan, has fortified the writers with care packages of scrumptiously edible goodies. Her father, Bill, at several points kindly offered to write the book for us. David's father, Farquhar, did his valiant, if unsuccessful, best to keep us on schedule with encouraging calls from Australia. To all these we express our gratitude and our affection.

—DANNA NOLAN FEWELL AND DAVID MILLER GUNN

INTRODUCTION

About the book of Ruth there is general agreement. It is an idyll, a brief moment of serenity in the stormy world of the Hebrew Bible.[1] Like so much other biblical narrative it is written, said the great German poet and critic, Goethe,

> in an exalted frame of mind and belongs to the realm of poetic art . . . [It] has as its noble purpose the creation of decent, interesting ancestors for a king of Israel; at the same time it can be considered as the most charming little complete piece of writing that has been handed down to us in epic and idyllic form.[2]

When the characters of this story are mentioned they are model characters who, in the best traditions of Israel's faith, act out the requirement of faithful dealing by God's people one with another. Above all, Ruth the Moabite woman is the one who shows Israel the way of faithfulness that leads to redemption. It was her "lovingly loyal behavior" (as one commentator puts it) that (in the words of another commentator) "brought back fullness of life to her widowed mother-in-law, Naomi, aided by Naomi's worthy relative Boaz."

We approach this story with several questions. What is "faith" in this story? What constitutes "faithful dealing"? What is "redemption"? And how does faithful dealing lead to redemption?

If faith has something to do with being "faithful," then at the very least it has something to do with a key word in our story, the Hebrew term *hesed*. "May Yahweh deal *hesed* with you (RSV: "deal kindly"), as you have dealt with the dead and with me," says Naomi to her two daughters-in-law at the beginning of the story (1:8). And later, confronted by Ruth on the threshing floor, Boaz speaks of her *hesed* to him being even

11

greater than the *hesed* she had done earlier, presumably in accompanying Naomi to Bethlehem.

Katharine Doob Sakenfeld's fine study of *hesed* in the Old Testament aligns *hesed* with the English terms "loyalty" and "faithfulness." Thus Ruth's *hesed*/loyalty to Naomi is seen as a model of "biblical faithful living" (1985:33). Commenting upon Boaz's speech at the threshing floor Sakenfeld writes (32):

> Ruth the Moabite woman is portrayed as the example of what loyal Israelite living ought to be like. . . . Her loyalty is then not just to Naomi (though that is primary) but also to her dead husband, dead brother-in-law, dead father-in-law—indeed, to the whole family of which she became a part through her marriage. Her "former" loyalty consisted in standing by her mother-in-law, Naomi, in coming to the strange land of her dead husband. Her "latter" loyalty follows through on the former in her initiative to provide an heir for Naomi (see 4:14, 17) and economic security for both of them within the structure of the system of levirate marriage.

That's a reading which has wide currency. But, then again, we might pause and wonder whether, instead of casting a mantle of approval over the story, it might not in fact cast a shadow. Is there not something just a touch bizarre about this model of loyalty, to a "family" which seems to consist, in essence, of so many dead men? To provide an heir for Naomi is Ruth's redemptive purpose—another male, that is, for the word "heir" masks "son." Naomi wants a *son*. What price, we may wonder (and the women at the gate echo our thought, 4:15), what price a daughter-in-law?

And what about economic security within the structure of the system of levirate marriage? "Economic security" masks, of course, the fundamental condition of this system, namely "female economic dependence." Another term for it is patriarchy; and it creates the conditions for this story. It is why both Ruth and Naomi find themselves destitute in the first place.

So are we then to view with equanimity, as the goal of model redemptive behavior, the restitution of that dependency? Faithfulness in the service of patriarchy. Put that way it sounds like a man's story. This, then, is a story that sits on a knife's edge. Remarkably for the Bible, it lifts up women as leading characters. Yet, in so many interpretations, the story's ultimate endorsement of the women seems to be that they serve the interests of men. That gives us cause to pause and wonder. Perhaps there are other ways of reading this text. Perhaps the idyll could be abandoned for a while and a leaner, tougher story read. Perhaps the notion of models of loyal living needs nuancing.

The history of interpretation shows us that readings of texts are usually built upon the readings of others. Ours is no different and has not been developed in isolation from interpretations of others.[3] No interpretation exhausts the text and there is always another reader to reinterpret some elements of the text and point out others that, this reader will claim, other readers who have gone before have missed. (Of course, the point applies equally to our own reading.) So we focus upon what we perceive other readers to have missed and try to account for as many of those "misses" as possible. Since most readers (though rarely consciously) miss elements that might subvert their understanding of the text, we, in picking up those misses, offer a (relatively) subversive reading—a reading that offers no model heroes, no simple messages, no unambiguous examples of how we are to live.

The reading we would suggest stems from a literary critical analysis. We read the text as we would a novel or a short story. We seek, for example, to be sensitive to shifts in the plot, to the unfolding of character, and to the play of language that both entertains us and focuses our attempts to find meaning in the story.[4]

We take the story world to be a realistic world, imitating our own world, peopled with characters who face the future with uncertainty, who do not know the end of the story. For narrative takes time seriously. Narrative is an art form which recognizes that meaning is never quite fixed, if only because time does not end, and a new possibility always exists, even if it be beyond the story's end. In order to appreciate the temporality of narrative, one might read as if for the first time, pretending the story is not as familiar as it is, and observing the sequence of knowledge as it unfolds to us as well as to the characters. The challenge is to not let our familiarity with the story keep us from being conscious of the way we constantly make and remake hypotheses about what is going on, why it is going on, who is doing what and why, and how it will all turn out.[5]

Besides being conscious of the way in which we as readers acquire knowledge in the story, we try also to be conscious of how the characters see events unfolding and how they acquire their own knowledge. What do they think is going on? What reasons do (or would) they give for the sequence of events? What do they know of each other? How do they think everything will turn out? In order to understand what the characters know, we listen carefully to their speeches, watch their actions, take note of the ways in which they respond to one another and, in all of this, try to be attentive to the sequence in which knowledge is disclosed to them. For the question of when characters know what is crucial to understanding their motivation and charting their development.

But just as our perceptions of real life situations are dependent upon context and point of view, so, too, do these factors influence our reading of mimetic narrative. People perceive and respond to the same circumstance in different ways. Readers are no different. Nor are story characters. In story, as in life, knowledge is like a prism—the light one sees is dependent upon context and the angle of view. So, in our story, a pious, but destitute and bitter, widow sees a different world than does a wealthy and well-respected male landowner. In fact, the perspectives of the narrator, the major characters, the community of the story world, and the reader all represent different sides of the prism. Hence, our reading is a play of perspectives, an attempt to see how each major character expresses faith, deals faithfully, redeems others and seeks redemption for him or herself.[6]

Of course, an even more basic question is how do we conceive of characters? Most of us have been taught in literature classes about "round" and "flat" characters, what Adele Berlin calls "full-fledged characters" and "types," adding a third category, the "agent" (1983:23-42). "Types" exhibit a limited number of characteristics and remain unchangeable and predictable throughout the story. "Full-fledged characters" are complex, multi-faceted characters who develop as the story develops and sometimes surprise us. "Agents" are "functionaries" who serve the interests of the plot and the characterization of other characters without manifesting character traits themselves.

While such categories, by alerting us to a range of possibilities, can usefully guide the way we read, they cannot be mandated by the text, only chosen by the reader. The range of data and inferences that potentially can be brought to bear on character construction may be considerable, infinite perhaps.[7] Selection is inevitable. Obviously a reader's ideological convictions will be influential. Often, too, literary genre shapes the choice,[8] without the reader being aware of the fact. Legends or fairy tales, for example, are often read in terms of character "types"—the brave young hero, the beautiful princess, the good fairy or the wicked witch—perhaps in response to the reader's sense of sameness in the telling of these tales. Yet genres are constantly being stretched and broken and every different text is potentially subversive of the genre. We can choose to read for sameness or for difference, to search for the complexity of characters or settle for types.

The reading of biblical narratives exemplifies the point. Generations of readers have come with a set of genre expectations (shaped by particular notions of the bible as hallowed and authoritative) that have excluded extensive character construction. Main characters, for example, have been expected to be either good or bad, models to emulate or abhor, "types" in fact.

We are interested in subverting the notion of "type" when it comes to biblical characters. We prefer, instead, to see the characters in Ruth as complex people, not merely built around a single primary trait, like loyalty, altruism or generosity.

Moreover, we try to entertain a play of coherence and difference. Character construction (by readers), like plot construction, is inevitably a search for consistency.[9] But underlying that search is often, not unreasonably, the notion of a single, consistent, definable "identity" or "self."[10] Reasonable or not, this is a problematic notion when speaking of real life persons. People may exhibit conflicting traits[11] and are often different people to different people. There is no reason why the same should not be true of literary characters. Accordingly we have tried not to define the "selves" of this narrative too tightly, and if we have overdetermined them, we recognize that as a fault. In short, the characters of this story have far more diverse possibilities of life in the minds of readers than we can ever give them.

For us, this text is a well-told story, complete with complex plot, complex characters and multivalent language. Because it is a story that imitates life, it offers us limited knowledge of the story world and no easy answers to the questions we bring to it.

The narrator offers us limited knowledge of the story world: doubly so, since the narrative style of Ruth, like much other Hebrew biblical narrative, is notably economical, laconic even. To understand the story we will have to be constantly filling gaps. Just as the unfolding of plot leads us as we read to formulate and reformulate hypotheses about what is going on, so, too, gaps in information—about relevant events, material conditions or what people know, think, and feel—lead us to construe what is missing in terms of what information we do have. It is as though we are invited to join the narrator in constructing the story. Careful and imaginative "gap filling" enriches the reading experience.

Some of our readers may already be having difficulty over the notion that such "gaps" could be crucial to an interpretation. The argument from silence has always been considered a weak argument. And anyway, the silences we perceive to be a force within the narrative may appear to other readers as inconsequential or simply not there. We rather suspect, however, that those readers who pass over these silences in silence have nevertheless interpreted them, even if unconsciously. Either they assume something about the character's attitude or about the story world, or they assume that they are reading a kind of literature which lacks complexity, where characters are flat and plots merely conventional.[12] But like intervals in music, gaps or silences in texts can carry as much force as do the notes or the words, as the case may be. We recognize the force of silence in life, where failure or refusal to answer may be of utmost significance. No less is true of our text.[13]

Interpreting silence, or "gap filling," is also a reason why the business of interpretation is never done. For there is no single way of satisfactorily reconstructing the information that we find lacking. There is always another possibility.

The story will admit of no easy answers to the questions we bring to it. We are, after all, dealing with narrative, not a theological treatise. And it is a complex narrative, even if on the surface it may appear to some readers to be simple. Its meanings are many, dependent as much on the perspectives (and questions) of readers as on the signs—the letters, words and sentences—on the page. There is no single "truth" fixed in the text, sleeping, as it were, and awaiting only the kiss of true interpretation to awaken it and give it life. To think of biblical interpretation thus is to subscribe to a fairy tale. If then, in our own reading we come to some rather confident-sounding conclusions, that is but a measure of our human frailty. We do not mean to smother the characters, overburden the meaning and leave the text a corpse fit only for burial. For we take seriously the notion of criticism as a process of engagement and reengagement, of evaluation and reevaluation.

We also recognize in the process of criticism that the reader's culture, values and emotions will be forcefully involved, wittingly or unwittingly. We have spoken something of this already. Our own investments in this text and in our reading of it are certainly more than we are aware, but one such investment that we would like to put up front—have already put up front—is our concern for some values that we might (loosely) call "feminist." These we are unable to disclaim in the interests of an "objective" reading; just as it is obvious that a "patriarchalism" implicit in many other readings over many generations has never been disclaimed by those readers.

Actually, the analysis does not spend a lot of time talking about feminism or patriarchalism, but rather expends energy wrestling with the world of the text in the text's terms. Yet even there our concern is obvious. The direction of our reading is shaped by major questions which women in our own society have raised against biblical texts and biblical criticism over the past decade or so. That is one of the conditions of our exegetical commitment, as we interpret a biblical text and speak of faith.[14]

Our book falls into three parts: Parts I and II and the Notes. In Part II we lay out the main lines of our analysis, shaping our discussion around the main characters. We start with Naomi, move to Boaz, then to Ruth. In the Notes are to be found references, minor points of exegesis, and discussion of some technical matters that are material to our reading but possibly more than many of our readers will want to be bothered with.

Part I is a retelling of the biblical story. Why? Our reasons are bound up with what we have just been saying about the nature of the narrative itself. No matter how cogently we argue our case in Part II, the analysis will remain ethereal, unreal, until our readers successfully accommodate it in their own rereading of Ruth. Talking about a story is no substitute for actually telling it. So what we are doing is taking a median position—retelling the story as we think it might appear to other readers who are rereading the biblical story, carefully and imaginatively—and in light of our particular analysis.

We have spoken of important aspects of the narrative: of narrative meaning as a product of temporal sequence and the play of perspectives; and of the elusive quality of narrative meaning, bound up as it is with imaginative reconstruction and the shifting contexts and questions of readers. How better to convey a sense of temporal sequence than to unfold the plot for ourselves? How better to explore point of view than to retell the story through separate narrators, each focusing on the story world through the perspective of a particular character?[15] How better to explore our interpretation while yet retaining the ultimate indeterminacy, the mystery, of the narrative than to retell the story in a more expansive style?[16]

We hope that our retelling will inspire other retellings. At the very least, we hope it inspires a closer examination of the text of Ruth itself. We hope, too, that it will convey our sense of biblical interpretation as a creative process. As teachers we have found retelling to be a liberating and enriching way of enabling members of a class to engage the text. A certain kind of understanding comes from looking at the text "from the outside in" (i.e. analyzing the text with any of various critical methodologies); yet another kind of understanding comes when, having done the analysis, one enters the text and "looks around inside" (i.e. empathizes with the characters and relates to their experiences). It is this second step that can engage and transform the reader.[17]

One last point. Why have we put the retelling first and the analysis second?

We envision the retelling as a tool that pulls readers into the critical process. Rather than simply reading someone else's analysis, readers are invited first to read between texts, so to speak, to compare and contrast our text with the biblical text. Readers can then make initial decisions for themselves, intuitively as well as intellectually. Does our retelling work? Does it fit? Does it help enliven and empower the biblical narrative? If, on the other hand, our retelling causes puzzlement, explanations can be sought in Part II.

In short, by putting the retelling first, we wish to assert that rationalistic, discursive analysis need not be the primary mode of critical exposition in biblical interpretation. We also wish to say to some of our readers—probably those for whom the sacred conventions of academia and exegesis exams are scarcely matters of high import—that if they are stimulated more by the first part than by the second, then we can live with that. They've probably got their priorities right. And their response is very biblical. For the Hebrew Bible is not exactly famous for an abundance of analytical, discursive texts. No, the narrative's the thing.

PART I

A
LAPFUL
OF
GRAIN

reading
ruth
in a
biblical
collage

ACT
I

BETWEEN
MOAB
AND
ISRAEL

PROLOGUE: JUDAH[1]

Watching his father grieve day after day was too much for Judah. Having these brothers around all the time didn't help either. He kept thinking about how they had all ganged up on that little preening peacock, Joseph. Joseph was gone now, but the presence of the brothers made it difficult for him to forget his own part in the conspiracy. Not that he cared about Joseph, but his father was getting impossible. He needed to get away from home. Maybe it was time he started his own family.

Putting some distance between himself and the clan proved less difficult than he'd thought. And the deal with Hirah the Adullamite fell into place easily enough, too. They pooled their flocks and Hirah provided living quarters.

It wasn't long before he decided he needed a woman. And he had seen one he rather fancied—the daughter of a Canaanite named Shua. That deal, too, fell into place. As did the children, three of them, all sons, which was good. Not that he was always around to welcome these sons into the world—there was that time when he was in Chezib.[2] At least he didn't have to explain what he was doing there. One thing about his woman, she didn't ask many questions. So what if business had a way of turning into pleasure sometimes.

He was ready to play father, however, when it came time for his sons to marry. God he was proud of those boys. Not a Joseph amongst them. So he took a special interest in finding a woman for his firstborn, Er. She would need to be a good looker, of course, but above all she'd have to have a strong build to produce strong grandsons. He had started dreaming of the line of Judah.

Tamar met his specifications. He made the necessary arrangements, saw her settled into the household and told Er to get on with it.

Instead, Er died.

It was a rather mysterious death not long after the marriage. He just dropped down dead. No reason.

That was a hard time for Judah, but he didn't waste his time grieving. He swore he would never be like his father, Jacob.[3] Life must go on. And for life to go on there must be sons. What to do? The answer lay at hand in time honored custom. Onan must take his brother's place. That way the line would continue to pass through the firstborn, at least in name.[4]

So he told his second son, Onan, to go into Tamar in order to produce a son for Er.

Onan didn't exactly leap for joy. Muttered darkly about secondhand pots.[5] Wondered aloud what was so special about Er's name that made it so much more important to preserve than his own. Judah ignored all that and told him to get on with it. And he did—well, sort of. Somehow Tamar remained decidedly unpregnant.

Judah had begun to wonder if something was amiss when, without warning, came the second shock. Onan died. He just dropped down dead. No reason.

No reason?

This time Judah moved more circumspectly. The two deaths could not be a mere coincidence. The common factor had to be the woman, Tamar. He didn't know quite what it was about her but he knew one thing for sure. Only a fool would surrender a third son to her.

Fortunately, Shelah was still rather young, so that he had an excuse ready if the widow should press him to honor the custom a second time.

And press him she did. It wasn't that she said anything. She just had a way of looking at him as if he should be doing something. At least that's how it seemed to him. She reminded him too uncomfortably of his father and brothers after the Joseph episode. It didn't take him long to tell her that she really ought to go back to her father's house and bide her time while Shelah was growing up and she was not to worry for when the time was right she could rest assured he would make things right. Shelah would do his brotherly duty by her. She could look forward to that son who was hers by right, that grandson that he so wanted her to bear for him.

That's what he told her, but it was certainly not what he thought. No way. The last thing he was going to do was to risk his remaining son in her lethal clutches.

And as he watched her pack her things he breathed a sigh of relief.

NAOMI

Elimelech didn't ask her if she wanted to move to Moab. In fact Naomi had some real reservations about going to live among those heathens. Moab, the children of Lot, a people born of incest, that's what she'd always heard.[6] But then they had those boys to take care of and there was no food in Bethlehem. No bread in the house of bread.[7] Hard to believe that the land of promise had become the land of death. And there was life in Moab, so said Elimelech.

So they packed their things and went to that God-forsaken place.

Elimelech was right. At least there was food. The boys could grow up free of hunger.

Naomi was just getting used to living in Moab, when Elimelech dropped down dead. Just like that. No reason.

Naomi was devastated. She also felt angry. She knew they shouldn't have come.

For a time she considered going back to Bethlehem, but for all she knew, the famine was still going on. Besides, what would her friends and family say. Served you right for abandoning the land of your fathers, the land of promise. Well, no fathers around now. They would have to make the best of it. The boys were about grown. Time they became fathers. No need to burden them with trying to raise families in a land of death. Better to stay put.

The sons took women for themselves—Orpah and Ruth, they were called—and though Naomi had reservations about Moabite wives, she was, in a way, glad for the company. There were times, however, when she remembered uneasily the story of Baal-Peor[8] that the priests used to tell. When she thought about *those* Moabite women, she got rather worried about her sons and about herself, too. If Yahweh were to know about these marriages, she feared, he might show his anger. Moabite women with their Moabite gods. She hoped her sons were staying faithful to Yahweh, but living in this place with those women, god knows it would be easy enough to forget who you were.

Ten years went by and Naomi's worst fears had not materialized. The family was managing to subsist. Nothing much extra, but they were surviving. What did sometimes worry her were the children—there weren't any. That barrenness raised from time to time thoughts of divine retribution and haunted her more with each passing year.[9] And with each passing year, her own sense of dependency upon Machlon and Chilion grew. She missed Elimelech. Damn him for dying like that and leaving her to grow old alone. But at least she did have sons, which was not true of everyone in the village—like her daughters-in-law, for instance!

Then they died, her boys, Machlon and Chilion. It was a terrible shock. Terrible. Dropped down dead, just like that. No reason.

No reason?

She knew they should never have come. It had been wrong from the beginning. Leaving their own folk, their native place, to live among these foreigners. Elimelech's death, the barrenness, now the deaths of her sons, both of them. They should all have gone back years ago when she had heard that the famine was over. The boys should never have married Moabite girls. They should have gone back home to find wives. That story of Baal-Peor kept pushing again into the forefront of her mind: "the people began to play the harlot with the daughters of Moab . . . and the people ate and bowed down to their gods . . . and the anger of Yahweh was kindled against Israel . . ."[10] Maybe Yahweh thought that that was what her family had been doing—playing the harlot, with the daughters of Moab, no less.

Not that they were evil women, Orpah and Ruth. Quite the contrary. They had been good to her and to her sons, loyal to a fault, even. But they were Moabite, nonetheless.

Now what? Probably had better not stay here, she thought. These people weren't going to take care of a foreigner and, without her sons, she had no means of support. Besides, if all this was Yahweh's doing, it wasn't likely that he would relent as long as she was here "playing the harlot in Moab." Would hers be the next death in Moab? Not hard to imagine, considering the situation she was in. Better to bite her lip and head home. She would simply have to take whatever her neighbors in Bethlehem had to dish out, be it ridicule or charity. She had no choice. She was alone.

As she packed her things, she met with surprising grief from her daughters-in-law. She had expected them to grieve for their husbands—that was only natural, but she had not expected them to resist her decision to return home. They followed her part of the way, as was the custom when seeing someone off, but when it came time for them to return home, they refused to turn back and created an awful scene.

"Go back," she said, "both of you, to your mothers' houses. May Yahweh be faithful to you as you have been to my dead ones and me. I pray that Yahweh will give you both a new home and a new husband."[11] And she dismissed them with a kiss good-bye.

The young women, however, weren't so easily dismissed. They wept aloud and insisted "No, we'll go back with you to your people."

Oh god, she thought, that's all I need! Yahweh on my back and these women as my shadow. To turn up in Bethlehem after all these years, in all this mess, and parade my mistake before the whole gate of my people. I just don't need them reminding everyone of where we went wrong. Elimelech and Naomi, the deserters, the ones who'd rather cast their lot with Moabites than stick with their own kind, stay with their own god. Finding food for herself, let alone acceptance, would be challenge enough. How could she deal with the stigma that a couple of Moabite women would bring? She just had to convince them to leave her.

"Go back, girls," she urged. "Why would you want to go with me? I've no other sons for you to marry. Go on back, girls. Go on, off with you. My husband's dead and at my age I'm not likely to find another. Even if I could find someone—which I can't—and if I got pregnant tonight, would you hang around and wait for whatever sons I might have to grow up? Would you refuse to marry if you had the chance? Of course not. No, my daughters, for things are even worse for me than for you, for I've got Yahweh against me."[12]

She watched them weep some more, her heart in her mouth. Then Orpah suddenly kissed her good-bye, turned, and began to trudge back home. But to Naomi's frustration, Ruth stuck to her.

Naomi found it hard not to show her impatience. "Look, your sister-in-law has had the sense to go back to her own folk and her own gods." The part about the gods slipped out. She hadn't meant to reveal her prejudice. She hastily added "Go on back after her."

Her words had no effect. Ruth started into a rejoinder. Her tone was determined. With sinking feeling and sudden weariness, Naomi knew that she would be stuck with her. She hardly heard the tumble of passionate words, only the end registered: "I'll be damned if I let even death separate us."

Naomi said nothing. She turned on the Jordan Road and started to walk, aware of the shadow moving along beside her. The journey was long, tiring, and silent.

When they entered the gate at Bethlehem, Naomi could feel the commotion their arrival had created. The word had obviously been passed along about the two women wending their way through Ephrathah, past the strips of standing wheat and barley, towards the town. A crowd of women had already gathered. She recognized some familiar faces, all of them older, too. Others, especially the younger ones, were strangers to her.

"Is this Naomi?" she heard someone say.

Naomi, she thought, my sweetness. That's what her mother had named her. How unfitting it seemed now. She turned to the speaker. "I used to be Naomi," she said. "Now, why don't you call me Mara. Bitterness, that's what my name should be." And she couldn't hold it back. The bitterness surged through her. And she blurted out, "Because El Shaddai has made me bitter. I went away full but Yahweh has brought me back empty. How can you call me Naomi as long as Yahweh is persecuting me and El Shaddai brings me nothing but evil."

The accusing words proved effective. She watched the shock register on some of the faces. And on others came looks of recognition. Silence fell. At least no one made any snide remarks about leaving Bethlehem and living in Moab. Surely these women should know that she'd really had no choice. And thank God no one mentioned the Moabite woman. She really wasn't up to explaining.

RUTH

When her father told her that she was to become an Israelite's woman, Ruth wasn't exactly ecstatic. That boy's family didn't have much, but then neither did hers. In some ways she couldn't believe that her father was selling her to a foreigner, but she guessed he thought that would be the best offer he'd get.

As it turned out he wasn't such a bad sort—her man, that is. And his family was pretty good to her, though she always felt that they all thought they were a little better than she was.

Nothing she could quite put her finger on, but she felt sure it was something about their sense of being Israelites. What was so special about being Israelite, she didn't know. But if it made them happy, so be it.

Life with the Israelites was fairly uneventful. She wondered sometimes why she never had a child and rather resented the unspoken assumption that it was her fault. Her sister-in-law didn't have any children either, though, and sometimes she wondered if maybe it had to do with these Israelite men.

Her mother-in-law, Naomi, was something of a superstitious woman. Her life hadn't been easy, that was true—she lost her man soon after coming to Moab. Ruth suspected, however, that Naomi never looked at that as one of those things. There was always some reason for death, something to do with the gods. Once, in a bad mood, Naomi snapped at her something about Moab being the problem. Ruth wasn't quite sure of the logic behind that, but it was clear that Naomi believed it. Ruth never pressed her to say anything about it. That wasn't her way.

As the years went by, she actually learned to love that funny little woman, with all her eccentricities. And she thought Naomi probably loved her, too.

Then everything changed. Within a matter of weeks both her man and his brother were dead. Just dropped down dead. No reason.

Ruth didn't think too much about reasons. She knew, however, that Naomi probably wasn't going to leave it at that. The gods at work again, no doubt.

The death of her man brought a kind of numbness to Ruth. She missed him, but sometimes she wondered if she'd ever really loved him. He'd never asked her and she had not really thought about it before now. She didn't suppose it really mattered now anyway. He was gone and she was alone.

Into the numbness broke the grim reality of destitution. She supposed she could marry again, but most of the men she knew weren't too keen on secondhand pots, especially if they'd come from an Israelite's cupboard. Of course she wasn't the only one left without a future. Her mother-in-law and sister-in-law were

in the same fix. In fact, things looked particularly bleak for
Naomi. Not only was she without her own menfolk, but Naomi's
father was long since dead and she had no other kinsman who
might feel obliged to take her in. At her age remarriage pros-
pects were nonexistent. At least Ruth could go back to her
father, though he would probably sell her to another foreigner
if he got the chance. A Moabite might not have her.[13]

She was still debating what to do when, without a word,
Naomi started gathering together her things. Not that she had
that much. She was, it transpired, leaving them. She was going
back to Bethlehem. Ruth couldn't really blame her for wanting
to go back home. Though there was little for her there, there
was nothing for her here.

Naomi set off one morning. Ruth and her sister-in-law,
Orpah, went along with her to see her on her way. When they
came to the boundary stone on the outskirts of the town they
stopped. Ruth watched Naomi and thought how tired and
defeated she looked.

"Go back," she said, "both of you, to your mothers'
houses."

Go back and find romance, courtship, marriage.[14] Ruth
wished it might be that easy. And then she heard her say
something about how loyal the young women had been to her
and to the dead men and then she started wishing them a new
home and husband from Yahweh. Not much chance, Ruth
found herself thinking. It would be her father who would find
the husband and who that might turn out to be, if anyone,
didn't bear too much thinking about.

Naomi and the dead men. Ruth heard that sound so loudly
in the middle of all that blessing. That's how Naomi feels, isn't
it, she thought. Like she might as well be dead.[15] Too bad
Naomi couldn't depend on that god of hers to be a rescuer.

Orpah was crying and Ruth found that she was weeping
some herself. "No," they began to insist, "we'll go back with
you to your people." The words probably came out as the
polite thing to say, but they stuck in Ruth's head. I could do
that, she thought. Why not? Nothing much for me here.

31

Ruth could see that Naomi wasn't buying their talk of returning with her, polite or no. "Go back," she heard her saying again. "Why would you want to go with me?" And then a convoluted speech all about how she was too old to have a husband, but if she could have hope—which she didn't—and if she had a man tonight—which she wouldn't—and if she bore sons for her daughters-in-law to marry—which she couldn't— the sons would be far too young and the daughters-in-law wouldn't wait around for them to grow up but would go off and marry someone else, anyhow. "No, my girls," Naomi conclud- ed, "for things are even worse for me than for you for I've got Yahweh against me." In this welter of "ifs" and "buts" and "maybes" was Naomi's loss again, the death of her menfolk. Husbands and sons, thought Ruth. That's all there is to life, isn't it. Husbands and sons and, of course, Naomi's god, the taker of husbands and sons.

Damn it, life could go on without husbands and sons. Ruth was sure of it. Fairly sure, that is. So when Orpah kissed her mother-in-law good-bye Ruth didn't budge. She had made up her mind. And when Naomi made some remark about how she should go back with her sister-in-law to her own people and her own gods Ruth smiled to herself: it's always religion, isn't it, Naomi—religion and country. Difference really does bother you, doesn't it. But now she knew exactly how to make her rejoin- der: "Stop telling me to leave you and quit following you. I'm going to go where you go. I'm going to stay where you stay. Your people can be my people. Your god can be my god." (That ought to get her goat, she thought.) "And I'll be damned if I let even death separate us." Death has separated you from all your men—everyone who counts—and you think that death is all that's left for you. If you go it alone, she thought, death will surely beat you.

Naomi made no response. But Ruth knew better than to think that her silence represented acquiescence. She could see that all her talk about switching people and gods wasn't com- pletely easing Naomi's anxiety, but her mother-in-law could hardly argue against her. If she'd been in her finest form, Naomi would have probably invented some other excuse. This time grief had drained her. Ruth had scored this one on Naomi's weariness.

Naomi said nothing else to her, though she matched Naomi's every step. It was Naomi's way of getting back at her, Ruth was quite sure. Since she couldn't achieve physical distance, she substituted emotional distance instead. So be it, thought Ruth. You don't know what to do with me and you're not really sure you care about me. That's all right, I remember when I wasn't quite sure I cared much about your son either.

The day they arrived in Bethlehem wasn't one Ruth cared to dwell on too much. There was talking at last—Naomi certainly broke her silence—but it didn't involve her. At least not directly. It was as though she was there but not there. There was tension between Naomi and the clustering women, and she knew she was part of the tension. Everyone was looking at her, though no one said a word. Yet Naomi talked as though she were invisible.[16] She felt accutely self-conscious, aware of her difference. In that moment, she'd never been so alone. Oh god, she thought, what have I done?

ACT
II

THE
HARVEST
FIELD

RUTH

They found Naomi's old house—Elimelech's house. It was not quite a ruin. There was enough roof intact to provide shelter and with work they could cut back the invading cactus, pull up the weeds in the floor, put stones back into the walls, make the place habitable. The first night it was enough just to clear out some of the other living things that had made the house their home.

The place took shape quickly.

In a day or two Ruth began to feel better about it. The trouble was that Naomi seemed unwilling to think of anything else. Nor did she make any effort to respond to the few neighbors who made tentative offers of help, bringing some food, an extra blanket, a water jar and cooking pots. Even the men who spent a day restoring the roof might well have wondered as they went home whether Naomi had really wanted them there at all. Did they remind her of the men she no longer had, Ruth wondered. For her own part, Ruth felt very awkward about the whole business. She tried to make up for Naomi's withdrawal, yet was conscious of her foreignness, her accent, the fact that it was Naomi these people were coming to see, Naomi's neighbors, Naomi's house, Naomi's town.

It was good to have somewhere to live. And people were kinder than she had expected. Ruth knew, however, that kindness was no substitute for security. Their food was running out, and no one was offering to go on feeding them for nothing. Neighbors soon got on with their own business.

Naomi busied herself around the house as though she expected a husband or son to return from the fields at any moment. Ruth had no such delusions. No man was going to set this new life in motion. They were on their own. Something had to be done. Ruth got up early one morning and said to Naomi, "I'm going to go to the fields today, if that's all right with you.[17] Maybe I'll find someone who is willing to let me glean[18]-." Naomi's response didn't surprise Ruth. "Go, my daughter," she replied abruptly. Go, thought Ruth, that's what you've wanted all along, isn't it. But this house and your memories of dead men aren't going to feed you.

She found herself beyond the town gate, looking nervously out over the fields of barley. She picked one at random.[19] Down the road, third on the left. She walked across the field to where the carts stood waiting to be loaded. She picked out the overseer from among all the workers and waited while he gave directions to the harvesters. She began to think she wouldn't be able to get his attention when he turned and saw her. He stared for a moment and his bold gaze made Ruth suddenly uncomfortable and more than a little vulnerable. She wondered what she was getting into.

She made her request to glean behind the hired workers. The overseer didn't seem to be in a position to give her permission and, for all his staring, Ruth thought he seemed a little embarrassed by his lack of authority. She would have to wait for the owner to come.

The owner did eventually arrive, just about the time Ruth decided she might better try some other field.

She watched as he rode onto the field. A man of importance, she could tell from his clothes and bearing. The workers looked up to acknowledge his arrival. "God be with you!" he greeted them. "And God bless you!" they responded. Naomi would like him, she thought, with all his pious talk. But maybe

35

it's more than just talk. His workers seem to respect him. He must treat them well. I hope his kindness also extends to strangers.

As he approached the overseer, his eyes immediately fell upon her. She felt awkward and looked at the ground. "Whose young woman is this?" Her flush deepened. Whose, he had said. Whose. Nobody's, she thought. Nobody's hired worker. Nobody's wife. Nobody's mother. Nobody's daughter. Nobody's sister. I suppose that makes me a nobody too. "It's the Moabite woman," she heard the overseer say, "the one who came back with Naomi from Moab. She wants to glean behind the reapers. She's been standing there waiting for you since early this morning."[20]

She looked up to catch his response. He was gazing at her, his head tilted. His mouth formed an ever so slight smile. "There's no need, my daughter, for you to go to another field. You may stay here and glean. Stay close to the young women who work for me. Don't lag too far behind them in the field. And don't worry, I'll see to it that the young men leave you alone.[21] So when you get thirsty, you can go and get a drink from the water jars that the men have filled."

Relief swept over her. She fell to her knees and bowed her head before him. "Why should you be so kind to me, sir? I'm a foreigner."

"I know who you are and why you are here," he responded eagerly. "I've heard all about what you've done for your mother-in-law since your husband died."

Since my husband died. Odd that he didn't say Naomi's son, she thought. Or Naomi's husband for that matter. Why should he bother to think of me as a widow? Why should he bother to think of me at all? But he's obviously been talking to somebody.

"You've left your family and your home," he continued, "and you've come to live among people you don't know. May God reward you for what you have done and may you find the refuge that you seek under the protection of God's skirt."

God's skirt! she thought. That's a funny way to talk about a deity's protection. Her eyes darted up to see if his expression might help her understand his words. His face was sincere. God's skirt. He must mean God's wing. I suppose the word can mean that, too.[22] The Israelites sure have a peculiar way of expressing themselves sometimes.

His blessing, despite its oddity, gave her the courage to stand. She struggled to contain her private amusement. She hadn't ever imagined herself being under God's skirt! What about *your* skirt she suddenly found herself thinking. She wondered about the nature of his interest in her. He didn't look at her like the overseer did, but he did look at her, intently. She rather liked his smile. And the tone of his voice.

"You are so kind to me, sir. You couldn't have said a more comforting thing. You touch my heart. And who am I? I wouldn't aspire to be one of your servants."

I might aspire to be something else though, she thought, if you were willing.[23] She glanced up at him and smiled. And as she turned to walk toward the harvesters she thought she saw the ghost of a grin in response. Was he reading her thoughts? Was he having thoughts of his own?

She worked for a couple of hours. The man's harvesters were awfully efficient. She couldn't see how she would have enough grain at the end of the day to make it worth her while. She rather hated the thought of going to another field where the reapers might be less thorough. And the man had offered her protection that she might not find in another field.

God knows what goes on out here during the harvest. And when you don't have a man for anyone to answer to? And when you're a foreign woman? She remembered the overseer's insolent stare. And she was becoming more aware of the reapers glancing back at her, murmuring to each other, laughing among themselves. Odd words floated back to her. "I could share a sheaf with that one," someone said. "She can have my stalk in her hand any time she wants . . ." "I could spill a little grain in her direction . . ." She thought again of the owner's first words to her. What was his name again? One of the young women had called him Boaz. Boaz. Anyway, she had been surprised when the owner had hardly spoken to her before raising the possibility of her being molested. Now she was beginning to understand a little better. Though whether his concern had been entirely on her behalf, she couldn't be entirely sure. Funny that such a matter should have been so immediately on his mind. She wondered again at the nature of his interest in her.

The workers eventually took a break, sought some shade and produced food and drink. Ruth hadn't brought anything with her. She'd been conscious of the larder growing empty.

The man Boaz called to her to join the others.

"Come have some bread and wine," he said. And he beckoned her to sit down among his workers. He passed to her the parched grain and she felt him watching her as she ate. His eyes smiled at her while the rest of his face retained its composure. You're a curious mixture, she thought. Pious. Restrained. Concerned about what your workers think, I suspect. But I think your blood pounds. I see it in your eyes.

She had more than enough for her meal and he urged her to keep what was left. She wrapped the food in a cloth, tucked it in her belt and went back to work.

As the afternoon progressed she began to find more and more grain, sometimes even whole stalks. The reapers seemed to have become increasingly careless. By the evening, however, as she beat out what she had gleaned and discretely compared her pile with those of the other women,[24] she began to suspect that her good fortune was perhaps not just fortune. Someone was looking out for her. It had to be the owner.

Naomi was, to say the least, impressed at the heap of grain dumped down in front of her. Ruth hadn't seen her so animated in days. Doubly so, when the younger woman brought out the food she had saved.

"Where on earth have you been gleaning? What have you got into? Someone's noticed you, bless his heart."

Ruth had to laugh. She had indeed dealt with someone who had taken notice of her. She told Naomi about him, adding finally, "And the name of the man I dealt with today is Boaz." Naomi's eyes lit up even more. "God bless him," she blurted out. "He's been faithful to the living and the dead." And she explained, "The man's a relative of ours. He's one of our redeemers."[25]

God's blessings and redeemers. Ruth smiled to herself. Naomi's world is filled with strange connections. Well, he redeemed us today, thought Ruth, but he's hardly likely to waltz through the door and put our lives back in order. A more hopeful Naomi, she thought, but a little naive. The grain didn't hop into the sack by itself. Men don't just notice you because you're needy. People don't just redeem you because they think God demands it and because they've got the wherewithall to do it.

Suddenly mischief got the better of her. "Oh by the way, this man Boaz told me to stick close to the young men[26] who work for him until all his crops are in." Naomi nearly choked on the bit of leftover bread Ruth had given to her. She struggled for composure and hastily said, "It would be better my daughter if you stayed close by his young women lest the young men molest you." Ah, so there is more to your world than God's blessings and men who come to the rescue. And do you now care what happens to me?

To Ruth it seemed that the conversation that evening marked a turning point in Naomi. Her anger against Yahweh began to dissipate. And Ruth herself felt her mother-in-law warm to her in a way she had not done before. Whether Naomi actually loved her or not, Ruth couldn't tell. She suspected that her presence still reminded Naomi from time to time of the death and destitution she had suffered. But with each day's produce she knew that her presence was coming more and more to represent life. She could tell from the way Naomi waited at the door for her each evening, that her mother-in-law was starting to recognize her worth. I may not be a husband or a son, she thought, but I'm the best you've got.

Ruth gleaned every day in Boaz's field. She tried not to think of what would happen once the harvest was over. She simply worked as hard as she could, taking advantage of every dropped sheaf, so that they could store as much grain as possible for the coming winter.[27]

On occasion she saw the man Boaz. The sight of him always gave her a curious thrill. He continued to speak to her with kindness. His eyes and smile attracted her but his pious words kept her at a distance. They were, after all, of a different class and of a different race and of a somewhat different age. She supposed all those things were important to him. So she honored his distance. But she often watched him while she did her work.

BOAZ

Boaz ben Salmon was an important man, a pillar of the community,[28] you might say.

He had plenty of property, plenty of money, plenty of respect. Folks admired him, looked up to him, sought his advice on personal matters, solicited his opinion on public affairs. He was a man of substance and the whole town recognized that.

He was one of the first landowners in Bethlehem to bounce back after the famine. That season, when the rains finally came,[29] his crops surpassed everybody else's. He provided jobs for lots of hungry people and helped many of the other farmers get back on their feet.

His success and generosity was not a source of pride, however. Well, not a source of much pride. He did give the credit to his god Yahweh, both publicly and privately. He truly believed his god was a god of goodness and blessing, a god of reward and protection. He knew this because he had experienced all these things. A little pride did creep in, however, when he thought of his standing in the community. He rather liked being held in high esteem by his neighbors. He rather liked having his workers look up in deference when he rode onto the field. He rather liked hearing their eager and respectful response when he greeted them each morning. He sometimes thought of himself as a hen with her brood of chicks. He rather liked that feeling.

Perhaps he valued all this because there wasn't much else. Besides his property, his money, and his reputation, there was little in his life. There was no one to talk to, no one to share with. He had been married once, a long time ago. His wife had died giving birth to their first child. The child, a son, lived for a couple of days, but then it died too. Boaz had never remarried. Sometimes he was glad of that, relieved that he had never had to feel such grief again. Sometimes, however, he was sorry about it. No woman with whom to share his success. No son to inherit his property. No grandson to keep his memory alive.[30]

When he started thinking like that, he turned his mind to other things. He didn't like feeling sorry for himself. He really had no right. After all, Yahweh had blessed him beyond measure.

He fixed his mind on Yahweh's blessing as he rode out to the field that first morning of the harvest. As he came down the road, he could see his harvesters already at work. The young man he had promoted to overseer was obviously doing his job well. He rode into the field and, as had come to be the custom, the workers straightened up to acknowledge his arrival. "Yahweh be with you!" he called to them. "Yahweh bless you!" came back the response. A good harvest this year, he thought. If all my workers stay with me, this might be the best ever.[31]

As he turned to speak to the overseer, he noticed a young woman standing by the carts. The Moabite woman. His dead kinsman's daughter-in-law. He had seen her from a distance, trudging alongside Naomi on the road into Bethlehem. That was the day they had arrived. He hadn't even recognized Naomi then—time had not been kind to her face. And, he had to confess, he had taken more interest in the younger woman. A woman of spirit, he had thought at the time, with a face and a form pleasant to look upon.[32]

The next day he had asked some of the townswomen about her. Not directly, of course. He had asked about the arrival of the two women the day before. He was surprised to learn that his kinsman's wife Naomi was the young woman's companion. Elimelech had died, the townswomen told him, and so had his sons. Naomi had come back by herself, they said. Well, except for that Moabite woman. The daughter-in-law. Mahlon's widow. Though what business *she* has here, god knows. Boaz had asked her name, but they didn't know. Later, he heard that her name was Ruth.

He gazed at her intently as his mind ran through these recollections. She shifted her weight from one foot to the other, looking somewhat uncomfortable. He wondered if anyone had taken her and her mother-in-law in.

"Whose young woman is this?" he asked the overseer.

"It's the Moabite woman," the overseer said, "the one who came back with Naomi." In other words, she still doesn't belong to anyone, thought Boaz.[33]

The overseer continued, "She's been standing here since early this morning, waiting for permission to glean behind your harvesters."

Boaz was thinking several different things at once.

For some reason he was pleased at the thought of the young woman's availability and he wondered momentarily what it might be like to have her himself. His mind was drifting over her skin, her hair, when alarm scared the fantasy away. Every other man out here is sure to be thinking the same kind of thing. While I could never act on my thoughts, others here would have no reservations about doing whatever they wanted. She has no man to protect her, no father, husband or brother for anyone to have to answer to. While these young men are good in many ways, they're not the most respectful of strangers. What they might not do to an Israelite woman, they'll think nothing of doing to her. After all, they're not likely to face any retribution.

His thoughts gave way to an insistent voice.

"Listen, my daughter," he heard himself saying, "you must stay here and glean. Don't go to anyone else's field. Stay with the young women who work for me. Don't wander too far away from them. Keep your eyes on the field lest your glances be misinterpreted. But don't worry about the men—I'll make sure that they don't touch you." The idea of touching her invaded his head again. "When you get thirsty, go ahead and drink the water that the young men have drawn. You'll be all right. I promise."

He watched as she bowed before him.

"Why should you be so good to me, sir?" she responded. "Why should you take notice of me at all? I'm a foreigner."

He couldn't help taking notice of her and being good to her, but he couldn't very well tell her that. A more controlled answer came out.

"I know you're a foreigner. I know all about you and what you've done for your mother-in-law since the death of your husband. You've left your father and your mother and the place you were born and you've come to a people you never knew before."

As he spoke the words, he knew they portrayed her somewhat heroically. He hoped she was flattered, but he also hoped she recognized his respect for her. Another father Abraham, he thought as he looked at her, leaving home and family and coming to sojourn among strangers. Except I can bet that no one made you any promises, did they? No one promised you a blessing. But I will offer you a blessing anyway.[34]

"May Yahweh reward you for what you've done. May Yahweh offer you protection beneath his wings!"

She arose and smiled at him.

"You have indeed been good to me, sir, for you have encouraged me and your words have touched my heart.[35] I am truly in your debt, though I would not be so always."

He watched her walk into the field. My words have touched your heart, have they? Well, yours certainly touched mine whether you intended them to or not. What a strange mixture of humility and boldness! Her gentle speech stirred him ungently.

At mealtime he beckoned her to join the others. She had brought no food. He guessed she had not had any to bring. She'd been working hard, but he could see that she wasn't collecting very much grain. He became concerned that she might leave and go elsewhere.

"Have some bread and wine," he said as she approached the group.

She sat beside him and ate with relish the food he offered. Probably the first decent meal she's had in a while, he thought as he passed to her some parched grain. She met his eyes with a smile of gratitude, relief and something else—he wasn't sure what. There was an openness about her face that seemed to reach toward him. He had never had a woman look at him that way before. He had never had anyone look at him that way, for that matter. He suddenly felt off balance and struggled to reestablish the proper distance.

"Work well, my daughter, and Yahweh be with you."

As she returned to the field, Boaz motioned the harvesters to wait. "From now on you will allow her to glean among the sheaves. Pull out some ears from the bundles if you have to and leave them for her to find. You will do nothing to shame her, do you understand? You will not disparage her in any way."

Some of the young men looked sheepish; obviously, they had already been making remarks if not overtures. Others looked amused. An old man's folly, he guessed they were thinking. But when they went back to work, they did as he had instructed.

The woman collected as much grain as she could handle. She was beating out her day's harvest when he left that afternoon. He was pleased to see how well she had done. She'll have plenty to eat now, he thought as he rode home, and she's not likely to go anywhere else to glean. I'll be seeing her in my field again. The thought made him smile.

NAOMI

Naomi sat rocking in the cool dark of the house. She wasn't really conscious of anything, not even the thickening darkness. She heard Ruth's footsteps on the path to the door. Oh, so you came back. Too far to walk to Moab by yourself? Then she remembered. The young Moabite woman had only gone to glean in somebody's field. I'm surprised some man didn't glean her. She peered at her daughter-in-law framed in the doorway. With the soft dusk behind her Ruth was merely a silhouette.

But she was a silhouette with a bulging shawl.

Ruth laid the bundle on the floor and walked across the room to light the lamp. The yellow light hit the yellow grain as she opened the corners of the cloth. Something inside Naomi began to stir as if from a deep sleep. She blinked to clear the cobwebs from her head. Ruth unwrapped a smaller bundle she had tucked in her belt. From it she took bread and parched grain and put the food in Naomi's lap.

For the first time in days, Naomi began to feel hunger. A hunger to eat, a hunger to know, a hunger to talk. "Where in the world have you been? Did you glean all this? You've lucked upon someone's generosity. God bless the man who has taken notice of you! Who is he?"

"I dealt today with a man named Boaz," her daughter-in-law responded.

Naomi's face brightened. She knew the man.

"Yahweh bless him," she murmured, "whose kindness has not abandoned the living or the dead."[36] That's us. You the living, me the dead. But we're bound together, you said so yourself. A kindness to you is a kindness to me. Yahweh bless him.

"The man is a relative of ours, one of our redeemers." Actually he was member of Elimelech's extended family, one of the ones who had done well for himself. He could afford to be generous on his dead kinsman's behalf.

She nibbled thoughtfully on the bread.

Her daughter-in-law was talking to her. "This man Boaz told me to keep close to his young men until the end of the harvest."

Naomi started. Keep close to his young men! Poor stupid girl. It's a wonder his young men didn't close in on you today. The man Boaz must have staved them off.

"It would be better, my daughter, if you stayed close to his young women, lest you be assaulted by the young men."

Ruth had averted her face so that Naomi could not see her expression. She suddenly realized that her daughter-in-law's remark had cornered her. She hadn't told Ruth about the dangers in the field when she left this morning and she had just confessed that she knew of them. Ruth was probably wondering why she hadn't warned her.

Naomi was wondering too.

ACT
III

THE
THRESHING
FLOOR

INTERLUDE: TAMAR

Tamar knew her father-in-law wasn't going to make good on his word. She had known it from the very beginning.

"Remain a widow in your father's house," he had said, "until Shelah my son is grown."

He could've stopped after "remain a widow" because that's what he had intended to happen. It wasn't her fault his precious sons had a way of dropping dead at the turn of a turban. Hadn't it occurred to him that maybe the gods weren't too pleased with the way his sons behaved? No, of course not, not Judah's perfect sons. They could do no wrong—not as far as Judah was concerned. But Judah didn't know everything. He certainly didn't know what took place—or didn't take place— behind the bedroom curtain after the sun went down.

Well, she had remained a widow in her father's house for quite a while, now. Shelah was grown, had been for some time, and Judah was doing his darnedest to ignore her very exis- tence. As for her, she wasn't getting any younger.

She would have to do something soon. She must have a son or else she would be stranded the rest of her life. Her father wasn't going to live forever. And she couldn't bear the thought of living on her brothers' charity and being the butt of their wives' ridicule. A child would obligate Judah to her. A son would symbolize to the whole community that she had a rightful place in that family.[37] Not that Judah's family was so great, but it was better than destitution.

On the day she heard that her father-in-law was going up to Timnah to the sheepshearing,[38] she decided that enough was enough.

His wife had died a couple of months before and, though he should still be in mourning, Tamar knew that a little thing like a death in the family wasn't going to keep Judah from having a good time. In fact, having done without his woman for a while, he was probably more eager than ever to find something or someone to make him forget his deprivation. Tamar was going to be that someone.

Not that she found Judah attractive. Quite the contrary. The thought of letting Judah near her made her sick to her stomach. But she knew she must have a child by some man in his family or else she could kiss her future good-bye.

She took off her widow's clothes and put on ordinary clothes—the kind she used to wear when she had a place in the world. With a veil covering her face, she waited beside the road to Timnah at the entrance to Enaim. She knew the impression this would make. Only a woman with nothing to do would loiter in such a public place. Only a woman *looking* for something to do and someone to do it with.

It wasn't long before she saw her father-in-law and his friend Hirah coming up the road. A stagger now and then gave away the fact that they had started the festivities a little early.

Just as Tamar had anticipated, Judah spotted her immediately. She could tell by his expression that he didn't recognize her, but took her to be a prostitute. He stopped in the road, whispered something to Hirah, and patted him on the back in a gesture to send him on ahead. Once his companion was out of earshot, Judah approached her.

"I want to sleep with you," he said abruptly.

Ever the charming Judah, she thought. Probably never even said that much when he had approached his own wife.

She mustered up a sceptical look.

"What's it worth to you?"

"A kid from my flock."

"I don't see any flock."

"I'll send it to you."

Yeah, I bet, she thought. Just like you sent your son Shelah to fetch me from my father's house. "I'll need a pledge," she returned.

He paused. She could tell that the negotiation was tougher than he had anticipated. "What do you want as a pledge?"

She had thought about this. "Your signet, your cord and your staff." Your identity, your bond, and your seed.[39] All those things you've withheld from me.

At first he hesitated, but then his hunger got the best of him. She knew that it would. She knew him pretty well. What Judah wants, Judah has to have. He took his signet and cord from around his neck and handed them to her along with his staff.

She led him to a tent she had pitched in a discrete, out of the way place. It was as dark as she could make it and she kept her veil on just in case he should decide to look her in the face. To her good fortune, but not surprise, he wasn't interested in her face. And thank god, it didn't take him very long to do his business. He was soon finished and gone.

As she watched him scurry furtively back to the path, she gripped his staff and silently hurled her words after him: Damned if I'll not get you a tribe of little Judahs yet. And damned if I'll not get me a place in the world. God, let me be pregnant. Let me have a son.

A month later she was sure she was pregnant.

INTERLUDE: LABAN[40]

Laban grinned every time he thought of his young nephew Jacob working so hard for his daughter Rachel. What a stroke of luck to have this love-sick pup hanging around, willing to do anything for the love of Rachel. The seven years of free labor was about to end—at least that's what Jacob thought. Laban, however, had other ideas.

The day Jacob came to him demanding his bride, Laban grinned again. Of course, he conceded, I'll prepare a feast. All the men must be invited to celebrate Jacob's taking of a bride.

Late into the night, after plenty of drink and bawdy stories, Jacob retired to his tent to await Rachel. Laban watched him lurch to his tent. What a gull, he thought.

Laban waited a few minutes, then went to his older daughter Leah's tent. He had told her earlier in the day to prepare herself to receive a husband. She had washed, anointed herself, and put on some of her best clothes. She was sitting, nervously waiting, when her father came in. I'm taking you to Jacob, he said. You are going to be his wife.

But Jacob loves Rachel, she began.

That doesn't matter, he interrupted. Now, you will go to his tent where he's waiting. No matter what, don't say a word. Do whatever he tells you to do. I'm giving you Zilpah to be your personal maid. She will come in the morning to attend to your needs.

He took her to Jacob and left her there in the darkness. He walked back to his own tent, grinning wryly to himself. Another seven years he figured. Seven years! It was a sure bet that Jacob would bargain again for Rachel—he was obsessed with her. And Leah? Well, Laban reasoned, whether she knows it or not, I've done her a big favor. She would have never caught a man on her own, not in the daylight. This way she's got a husband and she's no longer my responsibility.

Another seven years of free labor and a daughter out of the way. Not bad for a night's work. Laban went to sleep quite pleased with himself.

NAOMI

If life after Moab was actually going to continue, then it looked as though Naomi was going to have to give some attention to shaping what that life would be like. Her daughter-in-law had stuck with her and was obviously working hard to ensure their survival, but Naomi was finding it difficult to face a future of mere survival. She knew she could depend upon her daughter-in-law's loyalty: Ruth would see that she was taken care of no matter what. It really was a shame that she was a Moabite, though. If she'd been an Israelite, she might have received a marriage proposal by now from some eligible bachelor or widower—like the man Boaz for instance.

Judging from the amount of grain Ruth brought home every day, Naomi suspected that the man Boaz rather liked her daughter-in-law. She knew, however, that a man of his standing wasn't likely to risk his prestige for a bad marriage. He wasn't about to commit himself to a Moabite woman, no matter how attractive she was or how much he liked her. Well, he wouldn't commit himself *voluntarily*—but suppose he had no choice? Suppose it was a matter of honor. She bet that honor was pretty important to a man like Boaz.

The harvest was over and the threshing had begun. Naomi had heard that Boaz's harvest was now being winnowed at the threshing floor. She knew that it was a festive time for the men involved. Though the work was hard, it was nothing compared to the actual reaping. The men spent their nights there to make the most of the early evening and early morning breezes, and between evening and morning there was wine and laughter and stories before drunken sleep.[41]

The more Naomi thought about Boaz drinking and sleeping at the threshing floor, the more another thought kept coming to her.

She thought about the possibility of seduction.

If Ruth were to appear by his side in the middle of the night after he'd had plenty to drink, would he really ask any questions? There was no telling how long it had been since he had had a woman. An eager response in an inebriated condition and then, in the morning, he would discover the woman to be Ruth. He would rush through himself to justify this in the eyes of the community. An important man like Boaz would never let such a scandal stand. He would have to marry her—or at least pay her off. And if there were a baby involved, he probably wouldn't be able to resist taking Ruth, even if she was a Moabite, men being so obsessed with sons and all.

And whatever happened to Ruth, happened to her.

Ruth had said they were in this together. So, if Ruth acquired a home, Naomi would have one too. If Ruth found a man to take care of her, Naomi would have one too. If Ruth had a son, that son would sustain Naomi as well. Naomi's destiny was obviously tied to that of her daughter-in-law. Better make sure, then, that Ruth didn't take up with just any one. A man of standing, a man with money, a man with some tie to the family, and Naomi would have no more worries.

"Listen, daughter," she said to Ruth, "Isn't it time that I found a good home for you, that you might live the kind of life women are supposed to live? What about this man Boaz? I think he's rather fond of you. He's been letting you work with his young women and he is a relative of ours. I've heard that he is winnowing barley tonight at the threshing floor. Suppose you were to pay him a visit?"

She wondered if Ruth knew anything about seducing men. "Go, get cleaned up, anoint yourself, and put on your best clothes. Slip down to the threshing floor and stay out of sight until after the man has finished eating and drinking. Watch where he lies down for the night and then, after the others are asleep, go to him, uncover his legs, and lie down beside him. You don't have to say anything. He'll tell you what to do."[42]

She expected Ruth to resist the plan—it was, she had to own to herself, more than a little on the risky side; she also didn't know how Ruth would feel about this kind of deception. To her surprise and her relief, however, Ruth agreed to do it. Obviously she sees the wisdom in this, thought Naomi. She must know that her chances of getting such a husband in the light of day are slim indeed.

She watched Ruth disappear into the darkness. I hope to goodness the girl knows enough not to let anyone see her. If the men at the threshing floor spot her, they'll think she's come looking for trouble and they'll be more than willing to give it to her. Naomi shuddered and was suddenly glad it was Ruth and not herself having to make this little excursion.

She'll be all right, Naomi kept telling herself, and if she succeeds, we'll both be a lot better off. So, drink up, Boaz! And for God's sake, girl, remember some of the things that ten years of marriage taught you!

RUTH

Ruth hurried down the dark road, keeping in the shadows. Her heartbeat disturbed the quiet. Naomi is so funny, she thought, making this out to be all for my benefit. I know she's more worried about herself than me. Why can't she just admit it? And this Boaz scheme shows just how desperate she is.

By the time Ruth arrived at the threshing floor, the merriment there was dying down. The fire was low, the men were finishing their wine, and dispersing to find places to sleep. She saw Boaz in the soft fire light fill one more cup from the wineskin. He stayed up a little longer talking to some young men. She couldn't hear what they were saying.

Soon the others left to find beds. Boaz sat for a moment, staring at the embers. He drained his cup, banked the fire, and went and lay down at the far end of the heap of grain.

This was it. The moment of truth. She would soon know if Boaz's kindness was anything other than just kindness. She felt herself trembling. She took a deep breath and went softly to him. She uncovered his legs and lay down beside him. No response. Just deep, rhythmic breathing. He was asleep. She laughed to herself. Just my luck. I'm finally close enough to touch you and you don't even know I'm here.

She lay there in the quiet, feeling the rise and fall of his body beside her and thinking how nice it would be not to have to sleep alone again. But for now she wasn't sleepy. She listened to the night sounds and wondered what the night would hold for her.

She had been there some time—she wasn't sure how long —when she touched him gently on the arm. He awoke with a start. When he turned over, he was practically on top of her.

"Who are you?" He scrambled to put some distance between them and to cover his exposed body.

She thought of what Naomi would have her do at this point. Say nothing. Or perhaps respond something like, What does it matter? I'm here with you. Isn't that enough?

But Naomi's way was not her way. Boaz's decision would not be made for him. He would have to make it himself.

"I am Ruth, the woman in your debt." Her heart was beating fast. "Spread your skirt over me for *you* are my rescuer." You, do you hear? Not your god. I don't want your piety. I don't want your charity. I don't want your propriety. I want your closeness. Just once, try being close. You can trust me.

Silence.

She knew he could hear her words however he chose. He could take her tonight without any promise whatsoever and she would have no recourse but to do it Naomi's way. Any other man would do just that. But she hoped to heaven she had read right the looks he had given her out in the field. Surely he desired more than just a night with her.

At last he spoke.

"God bless you, my daughter. I can't tell you how much it means to me, what you've just said. Much more than anything you've done before. That you've kept yourself for me instead of someone more attractive, a younger man, whoever he might be. This is the most wonderful thing you could have done."

He paused. She felt him touch her face. "You mustn't be afraid," he went on. "All that you've said to me, I will do, because it is well known that you are a woman of character."

Ruth breathed a sigh of relief. I will do it because you are a woman of character. Just what she had hoped against hope she might hear. She expected that he would then "tell her what to do" as Naomi had put it. Instead, his low voice continued with words she didn't quite understand.

"Now it is true that I am a rescuer. There's also, however, a rescuer closer than me. Spend the night here and if, in the morning, he will rescue you then fine and well, but if he is not happy to do so, then I myself will rescue you. God as my witness. Lie here with me until the morning."

She didn't know what all this business about another rescuer meant, but she was pretty sure that it really had nothing to do with his commitment to her. He had promised he would take her for himself because she was a woman of character. To her, that was all that mattered. He had spoken to her heart. She moved closer to him and this time, he didn't move away.

She slept, knowing that everything would be all right.

He woke her early, before the sun came up. She arose, brushing her clothes, smoothing and covering her hair.

"Hold out your apron," he said. As she held it out, he filled it full of grain. He said nothing, but his touch reassured her. She left him in the dawn and made her way back to the village.

Her mother-in-law met her at the door.

"Well, my daughter, what happened? What's your situation now?"

Ruth smiled. Ah, but what you really want to know about is *your* situation. So she told her what the man had done to her, inviting her to stay the night and giving her the grain and all.

"He sent this grain back to you," she fibbed. "He said, 'You mustn't go back home to your mother-in-law empty-handed.'"

She couldn't resist the little jab about emptiness, remembering Naomi's speech the day they had arrived. She hoped Naomi was starting to realize that she wasn't empty after all.

She watched Naomi's face brighten. "Well, don't worry, my daughter. The man won't rest until the matter is settled."

BOAZ

Boaz felt good that night as he made his bed near the grain pile. He would make an ample profit off this harvest. The wine had made him pleasantly tired and he had hardly lain down before he was asleep.

Sometime later, in the middle of the night he supposed, he awoke, startled.

He felt the lower half of his body exposed to the night air and someone was close to him. Too close to him. He turned with a jolt to find a woman lying beside him. He couldn't see her but there was no doubt about her gender.

"Who are you?" he whispered with sleep in his voice. And he was about to follow with "what are you doing here?" when he was reminded of his bared legs. Obviously there's no need to ask what she's doing, he thought as he pulled his garments down over himself.

"I am Ruth," the dark figure replied.

He was stunned. Ruth. The Moabite woman of whom he'd grown so fond.

"Spread your skirt over me," the voice continued, "for you are a redeemer." Boaz tried to quell his excitement. He had desired her for so long and now she was here, inviting him to act on that desire. Or had he already acted on that desire? His excitement turned for an instant to alarm. He felt confused. All he remembered was the fire and the wine. He had to sort out her words. Spread your skirt over me, she had said. Surely this was an invitation. Her rearranging of his "skirt" had left no doubt that she was offering herself to him. But funny she should use that word. Maybe she means spread your wing. He remembered his blessing to her that first day in his field. He remembered, because he had thought about their first meeting a lot. He had said she would find refuge under Yahweh's wing, but now she was insisting upon his own wing.

Suddenly, it came to him. She's calling me on my words. Put your pious talk into action. That's what she's asking me to do. A blessing, he thought sheepishly, isn't a very adequate substitute for love. A blessing might be safer for me, but in reality, it means nothing to her.

Her words and her presence moved him so, he couldn't help but spill how he felt. "Yahweh bless you, my daughter, for this kindness surpasses what you've already shown to your mother-in-law. Instead of setting your sights on some attractive younger man—and there are plenty around—you've come to me."

This time, however, he didn't stop with a blessing. He found himself making a promise.

"All that you've said, I will do to you. For the whole gate of my people knows that you are woman of great determination."[43]

And soon, he thought to himself, the people themselves will know that you are a woman of worth. I'll see to that. You called

me a redeemer. That's got to be the answer. I'll redeem your
worth and I'll do it by invoking the redemption process.

He began to think aloud.

"It's true that I am a redeemer; there's also another redeemer closer than I am. We'll see if in the morning he is willing
to do a little redeeming. If not, then, as Yahweh lives, I'll
redeem you." He knew she wasn't following all this, but it
didn't matter. He knew what he was going to do, how he could
"spread his skirt" over this young Moabite woman with the
whole town's approval. She would look good. He would look
good. And they would have each other.

"Stay the rest of the night," he whispered.

He spent the rest of the night staring into the darkness,
conscious of her sleeping beside him. As morning approached
he had to wake her. No one must know that she's been here,
he thought.[44] But just in case . . . At his quiet bidding she
caught up the ends of her apron and he filled her lap with
grain.[45] If anyone should see her, they will think she has merely come here early to buy food. Careful not to wake any of the
sleeping men, he sent her back the way she had come.

Know, his thoughts followed her, that I mean what I have
said.

But then he wondered uneasily about what *did* happen
earlier in the night.

He dismissed the worry. It doesn't matter now. And he
laughed to himself as he planned the coming day.

ACT
IV

THE
GATE

TAMAR

O nly a matter of time now, Tamar thought, as she stroked her swelling belly. She had already been hearing the whispers in the streets. Judah will soon be told and he will be eager to be rid of me and to wield a little authority in the public view. Burn her! she could already hear him saying.

The day they came for her she was ready, a restless knowing had haunted her all morning. She finally saw them coming up the street. Nothing like a public execution to attract a crowd. She collected Judah's things from where she had hidden them for the last three months—his cord, his signet, and his staff. No one could mistake their ownership. she smiled a wry smile as she pictured his face recognizing his possessions.

They were pounding on the door. She gritted her teeth, squared her shoulders, and went out to meet them.

"Your father-in-law," said one, "has ordered that you be punished." Punished? she thought, that's putting it mildly.

"You," she said, turning to the voice, "you take these things to my father-in-law." She virtually spat out the title. "And you tell him that the owner of these items is the father of my child."

Those who were close enough to see the things recognized them immediately. First, silence. Then, whispers. Someone started laughing. Others quickly joined in. They cleared a path for her and she walked through them, following the cord and the signet and the staff to the town gate where Judah was waiting.

As she approached, he was given her message and presented with his things. She watched as surprise and then the deep flush of embarrassment took control of his face. The crowd was silent, eager with anticipation, waiting for him to find a response. Finally he cleared his throat and cleared her name.

"She is more righteous than I am because I did not give her to my son, Shelah." He never looked her in the face and she thought how typical that was of him, never looking, never seeing, never knowing, anyone but himself.

He hastened away.

I've always been more righteous than you, she thought, as he disappeared from public view. And now the whole town knows it.

BOAZ

By the time the sun was bright, Boaz was sitting at the village gate, waiting for his kinsman—the redeemer he'd spoken about—to pass by. That was a safe bet. Any man who was anybody came by the gate each morning to share any news, to pick up trading tips, to transact a little business, and mostly, to be seen.[46] Sure enough, there he was.

Boaz slipped to his feet and intercepted him as he headed straight for a little knot of men earnestly discussing the olive trade. Oh yes, I know, thought Boaz, you're anxious to sell that orchard of yours. Rather short of money right now, aren't you. And your dear Sarah is starting to ask awkward questions about the family business. Well, I'm really going to make your day!

"Hold it, friend," he exclaimed. Without giving him a chance to respond he steered him to a seat. "How about a word together?"

The man reluctantly pulled his eyes away from the olive men. He looked quizzically at Boaz, who gave him a smile, patted him on the arm, and, motioning him to stay seated, called to several other men standing nearby.

"A matter of business, friends; I need ten elders. Won't take but a few minutes."

He knew they would jump to; people liked to please Boaz. He was a wealthy—and could be a generous—man. And in a trice, there they were. Ten elders. Beyond their circle a growing crowd of the curious.

The relative shifted uneasily in his seat.

"Naomi," announced Boaz to the man, in tones loud enough for everyone to hear, "Naomi, as you know, has returned from Moab. Well, she's intending to sell the plot of land that belonged to our kinsman Elimelech.[47] So I just thought I should tell you about this." He paused and watched the man's face as he wrestled with this disclosure. Disclosure? Call it a white lie, thought Boaz with amusement. I'm sure Naomi won't mind.

There was a ripple of words amongst the crowd. He knew they were all sorting out the implications. By dint of the famine, Elimelech had left Naomi something of a liability where that land was concerned—and it was never much of a plot in the first place. The fact was, it was no use to her. Even if she were able to reclaim it, she couldn't afford to work it properly. By the same token, it wasn't a good investment to anyone else either, at least not short term.[48]

"The point is," he added as the murmur subsided, "You're the one who needs to redeem the land to keep it in the family. You are, of course, the closest kinsman. And we've got all the necessary witnesses here, so say whether you are willing to redeem it or not."

He paused a fraction, just enough to let the words sink in, not enough to let the man respond.

"And I need to tell you that after you I'm the one who has this reponsibility, and I want to know whether I need to redeem it or not."

The man was trapped, and Boaz knew it. With all those men sitting around, watching to see whether he would do the honorable thing, he didn't have a lot of choice. Nothing like a little ethical rivalry to keep the tone of the village high.

The man glared at Boaz. Nonchalantly—through tightened lips—he found the words, "Of course, I'll redeem it."

Boaz stifled a grin. Instead he merely looked pleased.

"Good," he said. "I, too, am going to do something for our family. On the day you take on Naomi's land, I've decided to take on Ruth the Moabite, poor Mahlon's widow, in order to raise a boy who will preserve the dead man's name and inheritance."[49]

This time the murmur was a babble. "Did you hear that!? Can you believe it? Never heard of a man volunteering to do that if he didn't absolutely have to. And, good lord, he's marrying a Moabite woman! Good for Boaz. You know, he always does the right thing. Now that I call generous—a pity Mahlon's not here to see what he's doing for him."[50]

Boaz watched his man's face turn from disbelief to panic mixed with anger.

That he knew Boaz had trapped him was plain. And Boaz knew exactly what he was thinking. It was bad enough to be forced to tie up the money (and ruin the point of the olive tree sale!). But to do that on a long term investment and then have the property revert to some boy who would go by the name of Elimelech but who would really belong to Boaz— that was different, that was altogether too much. All the man could do now was retreat as gracefully as his embarassment would allow.

"I can't redeem it for myself," he muttered. "That would damage my own estate for my own son. You take my right to redeem. Do it yourself. I can't redeem it."

And with that he pulled off his sandal to hand it to Boaz in symbolic acknowledgement of the transfer.[51]

Right to redeem? Obligation to redeem, is more to the point, thought Boaz as he took the sandal. He returned the man's resentful gaze with equanimity and soaked up the patent admiration which the crowd exuded. No doubt about it, one always looks better when someone else looks worse. It was time to effect some formal closure.

"You are witnesses today," he announced, including in the sweep of his gaze the whole assembled throng—nothing like making those on the fringe feel as though they belonged where the action was. "You are witnesses today that I have taken on from Naomi all that belonged to Elimelech and all that belonged to Chilion and Mahlon. Also, I have taken on Ruth, the Moabite woman, to be my wife, to perpetuate the name of the deceased, Mahlon, by keeping open his line of inheritance, so that the name of the deceased man may not disappear from among the men of his family and from the public places of his native town. You are witnesses today!"

Well they loved it, of course. Every father's son of them loved it. Boaz just knew he had them in the palm of his hand. First to offer to do the redeeming. Nothing like property to grab men's interest. Then all that wonderful stuff about dead men's names continuing on and preserving inheritances for sons. Old Ahithophel ben Hushai jumped up to his feet at once—Boaz could have predicted it—and launched into a florid response. Boaz bowed his head in appropriate humility and heard the words float serenely around him:

"We are indeed witnesses," began the elder. "And I'm sure I speak for everyone here"—and his gaze took in the whole assembled throng—"when I pray that Yahweh will see to it that the woman who is coming into your house be like Rachel and Leah, who, in harmony, built the house of Israel.[52] May your wealth increase in Ephrathah. May your name be honored in Bethlehem. May your house be like the house of Perez, the son of Judah by Tamar, because of the seed that Yahweh will grant you by this young woman."

Great acclamation greeted the speech. Boaz was surrounded by well-wishers and it was some time before he managed to extricate himself, make for home, send a message to Ruth, and set in train the necessary arrangements.

Only later did he reflect on old Ahithophel's words.

That the elder should fix on the story of his ancestors, Judah and Tamar, to flatter Boaz was wonderfully ironic. How could anyone know how close they might have come to proclaiming, like Judah's neighbors, "Ruth, your kin-in-law has been sleeping around and got herself pregnant."

Nor could he let on how he had said to himself over and over, lying on the threshing floor with Ruth asleep beside him,

"It has taken this young Moabite woman to show me the right thing to do."

And Leah! He laughed at the thought of Naomi as a female Laban, scheming to get Jacob's support by smuggling Leah into the younger man's bed under cover of darkness and, doubtless, no little drink.

His thoughts turned to the future.

Perhaps one day the townspeople would really come to accept Ruth for herself, worth something in her own right, not just because she was a channel for a son, a substitute Mahlon. Perhaps then he might be able to share his story across a winter's fire, or maybe out under the stars, in the warmth of a summer's evening, by the threshing floor, at the edge of the heaps of grain.

He thought of the grain, the seed, and all that talk about sons. As though there were nothing to it. He would have all these sons. They had all slapped him on the back and told him to get on with it.

He thought of the cold on his legs, of the young woman lying close, warm. He felt an ache for her. He wanted her breath on his cheeks. And then he felt suddenly old. He had conjured her Moabiteness away. But would not age divide them? From the beginning he had been conscious of his age. "My daughter," he had called her. But she had said, "Spread your kanaph." He hoped that she really did want him.

When it was time, Boaz tried not to let his nervousness show.

EPILOGUE

THE MIDWIFE

The midwife hurried down the street to Judah ben Jacob's household. His daughter-in-law was about to deliver. Funny business, this, a daughter-in-law giving birth to a father-in-law's baby. Still, you have to admit, the woman had guts and it paid off. This Tamar now has a home—such as it is—and security. Let's hope that the baby is a boy, then Judah will make sure Tamar never has any worries.

The labor was long because there were two babies instead of one, and they couldn't seem to decide which one would be born first. At one point a tiny fist appeared and the midwife tied a red string around the wrist to indicate that this one was the first born. But, lo and behold, the fist withdrew and the other baby pushed its way out first. Well, mused the midwife, aren't you a pushy little fellow! Take after your mother, do you? We'll have to name you Perez, since you're the one who burst out first.

The other baby was also a boy.

"Well, young lady," said the midwife, "you did yourself proud. Two sons who will look after you in your old age."

Tamar managed a feeble and relieved smile and, holding the two boys, drifted off to sleep.

In later years, the midwife often thought of the determined young woman who had made a place for herself in society by pushing her way into Judah's family, and the son who had pushed his way into the world ahead of his brother. What a strange story. She sometimes heard folks speak of Judah and his sons. But there never was much mention of Tamar. She always wondered what had happened to her. What had her life been like? Had it all be worth it?

THE NEIGHBORHOOD WOMEN

The news that the Moabite woman was pregnant occasioned no little comment in the neighborhood.

The doubters who had thought she was probably barren and Boaz out of luck had to eat their words. Naomi's near relative privately congratulated himself on his decision to retreat on the redemption deal—which, however, did not stop him resenting the way things seemed always to fall out right for his wealthy kinsman. Boaz's friends all came by to drink to his health.

Naomi's friends congratulated her and talked about what the boy should be called. They all assured her it would be a boy—a boy to carry on Elimelech's legacy, a boy to take care of her in her old age. They enjoyed seeing her smile so much.

One or two of the women hoped among themselves that Naomi would keep some things in perspective. Her position in the household was delicate. The birth of a child could complicate things. They hoped that the older woman and her young companion wouldn't find themselves struggling for control. The child—if it were a boy—would be Naomi's redeemer, but also Ruth's son. Two mothers in one household was bound to produce trouble, they thought.

Someone recalled old Ahithophel's speech at the gate about Rachel and Leah and volunteered the view that whatever building they had done it hadn't exactly been "in harmony." And look at the stories of Sarah and Hagar and all the bitterness that a pregnant surrogate caused. There was a moral in those old tales. Fertile women and barren women don't get along too well in the same household.

Not everyone saw contention ahead for Naomi and her daughter-in-law. Nevertheless, recall of the old stories did rather put a damper on the idea that Naomi would actually be treated as the child's mother or even paternal grandmother. After all, Hagar's child was never really considered to be Sarah's. Nor were Bilhah's children thought to be Rachel's.[53] Fictions through surrogacy were never quite believable, especially when the woman who had given birth continued to live in the same household.

It was a boy.

Naomi showed him off to all the women who came to visit. All the appropriate things got said. Suitable words of blessing were addressed to God for arranging things so satisfactorily for Naomi. She was not to be left without a redeemer, someone to give life back to her, to keep her as she grew old. What a name he would have in Israel. And the women gave him that name. Obed. Naomi's son.[54] Their words matched her mood. She was so proud of the boy.

Some other words found their way through the excitement and the congratulations and the blessings.

"Your daughter-in-law who loves you is more to you than seven sons," someone ventured.

Naomi ignored the remark and put the child to her breast.

DRAMATIS PERSONAE

LABAN. A trickster. Who sold his daughter to a life of unhappiness, for seven years of labor.

JUDAH. A man who took what he wanted. Who was proved unrighteous by the woman he thought to discard.

TAMAR. A woman who redeemed herself through uncommon means. A survivor.

PEREZ BEN JUDAH. The son Tamar bore to Judah. The unexpected one.

ELIMELECH. A man who went to Moab. And died.

CHILION. A son of Elimelech. Who married a Moabite woman. And died.

MAHLON. Another son of Elimelech. Who married a Moabite woman. And died.

Boaz. A man of substance. Who enjoyed public favor. Who had a soft spot for a Moabite woman. Who married her—in order to perpetuate the name and property of a dead man, Mahlon. Or so he said.

NAOMI. The widow who tried to leave Moab behind her. Who first counted herself among the dead. Who found life in a lapful of grain, the labor of her daughter-in-law, a son.

OBED BEN BOAZ. The son born to Naomi. The son the Moabite woman bore. The son of Boaz's old age, born to raise up the name of a dead man. Whom, after a while, nobody remembered was meant to be the dead man's son. Who was just called after his father as usual. Even the town records named him that way. (According to the records, the grandfather of King David.)

RUTH. The Moabite who followed Naomi back from the fields of Moab. Stayed among people not her own. Fed her mother-in-law. Loved the man called Boaz. Brought life into the world.

THE END

PART II

GLEANING
THE
FIELDS

a
literary-
critical
reading
of
ruth

1

NAOMI
THE
WIDOW
OF
ELIMELECH

THE SETTING: ISRAEL AND MOAB

We begin with the setting of the story. Bethlehem—the house of bread—is suffering a famine. Elimelech and his family leave home to find food in Moab. What is the significance of Moab? Why not Egypt, Edom, Paddan-Aram, Philistia? What connotations does Moab carry for the Hebrew characters of the story, and how might a Hebrew audience feel about Moabites?

The story of Lot and his daughters (in Genesis 19), when read through an ethnic lens, suggests, for a start, that feelings of moral superiority, a righteous chauvinism, might be characteristic of attitudes to this near neighbor. While the Israelites were the descendants of divine promise and miraculous union, the Moabites were the descendents of deception and incest.[1]

Deut 23:2-4 [Heb. 3-5] carries a negative memory of Moab's role in Israel's advance toward the promised land and insists that prohibition should keep that memory fresh:

No child of incest shall enter the assembly of YHWH; even the tenth generation shall not enter the assembly of YHWH. No Ammonite or Moabite shall enter the assembly of YHWH; not even the tenth generation shall enter the assembly of YHWH, for ever, because they did not meet you with bread and water

on the journey, when you came out of Egypt, and because
they hired against you Balaam . . . to curse you.

The actual story of Israel's dealings with Moab during the
approach to Canaan suggests even stronger reasons for Israel's
later reluctance to get too close to Moabites, particularly Moabite women:

> So Israel dwelt in Shittim and the people began to play the
> harlot with the daughters of Moab, who invited the people to
> the sacrifices of their gods. And the people ate and bowed
> down to their gods. So Israel yoked itself to Baal of Peor and
> YHWH's anger burned against Israel; and YHWH said to Moses,
> "Take all the leaders of the people, and hang them for YHWH
> in broad daylight, that YHWH's burning anger may turn away
> from Israel." (Num 25:1-4)

So Elimelech sets out to find food, to *eat* in Moab! Not, perhaps, the most propitious beginning to a story.[2]

NAOMI LOSES HER MEN

Indeed, once in Moab, Elimelech dies and Naomi is left with her
two sons. These take Moabite wives, Orpah and Ruth. After
living there some ten years the sons, too, die, "so the woman
was left without her two boys and her husband" (1:5).

The woman has heard that there is again food in her home-
town of Bethlehem. With no husband or sons, there is no
reason for her to stay in Moab. And with no husband or sons,
she makes her own decision to return. Although her daughters-
in-law accompany her part of the way, Naomi soon tries to send
them back to their own homes (1:8-9).

> Go, return, each of you to her mother's house.
> May YHWH deal *hesed* with you
>   as you have dealt with the dead ones and with me.
> May YHWH grant that you find security,
> Each in the house of her husband.

Naomi's speech begins to reveal who she is and what she is
thinking and feeling. To be sure, the surface rhetoric is directed
outward to the young women; she wishes the best for them. She
hopes that YHWH will be faithful to them and that they will find

new homes and husbands. But at the heart of this speech, indeed, at the heart of all her utterance in this chapter, is Naomi's bitter sense of deprivation. She equates herself with the dead ones.

Language has a way of doing more than it says. No less is true of Naomi's speech. As she urges them toward their mother's houses to find new husbands, her language communicates that they have options. She does not. As she piously wishes that God deal faithfully with them, she is pointing to the fact that God has not dealt faithfully with her. The young women, not YHWH, have shown her kindness. Indeed, as Trible has observed "these female foreigners become models for Yahweh. They show the deity a more excellent way" (1978:170).

Although she dismisses them with a kiss, they lift their voices in weeping and protest: "No, we will return with you to your people." Naomi, however, is insistent (1:11-13):

> Return, my daughters, why go with me?
>> Have I any more sons in my belly
>> for you to have them for menfolk?
> Return, my daughters, go,
>> for I am too old for a man to have me.
>>> What if I thought there was hope for me,
>>> even if a man should have me tonight,
>>> and even if I bore sons?
>> So then you are going to wait till they have grown up?
>> So then you are going to shut yourselves away,
>>> so that a man cannot have you?
> No, my daughters,
>> for it is much more bitter for me than for you,
>> for the hand of YHWH has gone out against me.

In this second speech repetition, hypothetical situation, and climactic closing statement shape the rhetoric. The emphasis falls upon men (husbands) and sons. While on the surface Naomi's concern is for the young women, that is, providing men for her daughters-in-law to marry, her deeper problem is that, having no man herself, she can never again have sons. Her speech to the daughters wears the younger women on its sleeve. They may have hope, she has none. The final statement makes her perspective clear: things are far more grim for her than for these two young women.[5]

NAOMI AND YHWH:
THE PROBLEM WITH MOABITE WOMEN

In Hebrew her speech ends with "the hand of YHWH." Here her emptiness, her loss, comes to rest at YHWH's door. What does she mean? Why does she think that YHWH is against her?

Allusion may help us construct an answer. We have indicated how Moab might have been regarded with some suspicion by this Bethlehemite. If the story of the men at Shittim were part of her heritage, we can imagine with what apprehension she might have viewed her family's moving to Moab, and how much more so her sons' marrying Moabite women. Might not that entanglement with Moab be construed by Naomi as the reason for the deaths that had struck her men, the sign of God's hand against them, against her?[6]

Her outcry, "the hand of YHWH has gone out against me," is, of course, ambiguous. Does she see herself as the innocent victim of the men's transgression? Or does she herself share the guilt and thus the punishment? Perhaps, confused and distraught in her grief, she allows both possibilities to haunt her.

Allusion to Moab, therefore, may help us understand Naomi here. So may another important allusion.

NAOMI AND JUDAH:
DANGEROUS LIAISONS

The exposition describes a situation structurally reminiscent of the exposition to the Judah-Tamar story (Genesis 38). There is a separation from family/homeland because of an unpleasant situation,[7] a sojourning elsewhere, marriages to foreign women, deaths of spouse and two sons—all told in rapid succession.

The similarities invite a comparison between the characters of Judah and Naomi.

In many major respects the two characters are vastly different. Judah is very much in control of his life and his family. He initiates his move from home. He arranges his sons' marriages.

As a man his identity and security are bound up to some extent with his sons (lineage and name) but not at all with his spouse. He greets the deaths in his family with little grief and overriding pragmatism. He has options: one can always secure another woman who will have other sons.

Because Naomi is a woman, her loss is more poignant. It is not she, but her husband who, until his death, controls her life and family. Her husband has brought her to Moab. As a widow she is dependent upon her sons for economic security and the text indicates that the sons arrange their own marriages. Her opinion of these matches is neither consulted nor revealed. When her children die, the narrator says that she is "left over" (*vattissa'er*), left alone. By her own admission, she has no hope for either another husband or more sons.

Though her situation is more devastating than that of Judah, Naomi, like Judah, analyzes the reasons for her tragedy. As we have observed, her voiced conclusions indicate that God has caused her misfortune. Although unvoiced, the sojourn in Moab and the marriages to Moabite women appear to be feasible explanations why she might conclude that God has seen fit to treat her so. The allusion to Judah's story, moreover, sharpens our reading. Attention to this story suggests that Naomi, like Judah, perceives the women to be at the heart of her predicament.

In the Judah-Tamar story Judah regards Tamar the Canaanite with suspicion, considering her to be the cause of the trouble (namely, the deaths of his two sons). He does not accuse her of this openly, however; rather, he urges her to return to her father's house.

Naomi's attitude towards her daughters-in-law is cloaked by an ambiguous text; but she does urge them insistently to return to their mother's houses. The allusion to the Genesis tale prods us. Might she perhaps be like Judah? Might she be veiling her suspicion of the young women, but insisting nevertheless that they belong not with her but with their own families in Moab? Ruth and Orpah, then, would be to Naomi like Tamar is to Judah—an albatross around her neck.

Read thus, her blessing is two-edged. "May YHWH deal
hesed with you . . . . May YHWH grant that you find a home"
(1:9). The words may well convey her recognition that the
women have treated her kindly. At the same time they are a
way of distancing herself, as they wrap in piety her message to
them to part from her. But even the piety is a little strained—for
her perception is that these Moabite women have their own
gods (cf.1:15—"See, your sister-in-law has gone back to her
people and her gods"). We sense the possibility that her verbal
generosity is but polite rhetoric.

NAOMI AND THE MOABITE WOMAN

Naomi ceases to speak

In the exchange between Naomi and the daughters-in-law in
chapter one, Trible observes that, ironically, Ruth's unity with
Naomi stems from her opposition to her: "Ruth's commitment
to Naomi is Naomi's withdrawal from Ruth" (1978:172-173).
But *why* does Naomi so withdraw, if she is so selfless, so wholly
motivated by her regard for others as Trible's reading would
have it? "Throughout the exchange," writes Trible, "[Naomi's]
counsel is customary, her motive altruistic, and her theology
tinged with irony" (171).

Let us accept the conventional counsel and the caustic
theology. But why should the altruism of Ruth reduce an altruistic Naomi to silent withdrawal? "She ceased to speak to her"
says the Hebrew text. Indeed she speaks not a word either to,
or about, Ruth, from this point to the end of the scene in the
arrival at Bethlehem. If Ruth's famous "Where you go, I go . . .
your god, my god" speech can melt the hearts of a myriad
preachers and congregations down the centuries, why not
Naomi's heart?

In our reading, Naomi's silence at Ruth's unshakable commitment to accompany her is not unexpected. Naomi is attempting to shake free of Moab and the calamity she associates with
that place and its people. Resentment, irritation, frustration,
unease may well lie behind her silence. Ruth the Moabite may
even menace her future.

Naomi returns empty

Naomi's withdrawal from Ruth is particularly marked in the scene of arrival among the women of the town.

Responding to the women's exclamation, "Can this be Naomi?" she retorts (1:20-21):

> Do not call me Naomi,
> call me Mara,
> for Shaddai has made me very bitter.
> I went away full,
> YHWH has brought me back empty.
> Why call me Naomi,
> when YHWH has afflicted me
> and Shaddai has caused me evil?

The speech is a series of polarities: sweetness (*na'omi*) has turned to bitterness (*mara'*); fullness has become emptiness; delight (*na'omi*) is now evil. And through the entire speech, Naomi herself (signaled by the repetition of "me") is the object of divine wrath. Her worldview is theistic. She ascribes her calamity to YHWH and her language echoes that of Job.[9]

She had gone away full, she proclaims (discounting the famine). She has been brought back empty. She has lost her men. The trip to Moab has been a disaster. Her departure and return thus frame the source of her problem, the unvoiced implication: living in Moab and cohabiting with Moabites.

She went away full, was returned empty. She sees herself alone, apart from a vengeful God. The implication for Ruth is devastating. Ruth is nothing. Naomi speaks as though the loyal companion at her side were invisible.[10] Ignoring the younger woman before the women of the city, Naomi expresses in her silence her resentment, perhaps. Perhaps, too, her silence about Ruth is the silence of embarrassment. The Moabite who stands alongside her embodies Naomi's (though in actuality Elimelech's) abortive flirtation with foreignness.

At the heart of Naomi's speech, then, is Naomi, her grief, and her sense of victimization, guilt and helplessness. Ruth is found only in the silence. Little wonder that, as chapter 2 begins, still the only words she can find for her daughter-in-law are "Go, my daughter!" (2:2), echoing her insistence earlier on the journey: "Go! Return (1:8) . . . Return! (1:11) . . . Return! Go! (1:12) . . . Return! (1:16)."

NAOMI AND THE BREADWINNER

Naomi and Ruth's security: at risk in the field

A Naomi who is jaundiced about foreigners, a Naomi who thinks like Judah, is also consistent with a Naomi who sends Ruth to the harvest field without advice or warning.

The field is a place of some menace for an unattached young foreign woman (note the narrator's reiterated epithet for Ruth, "the Moabite woman"). We find in Boaz's speeches repeated reference to the risk Ruth runs from the men (who are, in the Hebrew, carefully distinguished from the women), namely the risk of unwelcome attention and molestation, that is, sexual assault.[11]

His first words to Ruth directly address the problem. "Listen here, my daughter, you are not to go gleaning in any other field. Truly you are not to go on further from here, but stick with my young women. Keep your eyes on the field being harvested, and follow them. Won't I see to it that the young men do not molest (ng') you?"[12] Again in vv. 15-16 Boaz warns his men against interfering with Ruth, "Let her glean even among the sheaves, and don't interfere (klm) with her. And what's more, you're to pull from the bundles for her, and leave her alone[13] and let her glean, and don't harass (g'r) her."[14]

The risk of harrassment is something of which Naomi herself is aware. At the end of Ruth's first day in the fields, when Ruth, perhaps teasingly, reports that Boaz had urged her to stick close to the young men, Naomi replies belatedly that it would be better if she went out with the young women,[15] lest she be assaulted (pg') in another field (2:22).[16] Why did Naomi not warn Ruth before she left that morning? Why now the sudden concern? Because Ruth has become her bread-winner? Because she has sensed the possibility of bounty near at hand (through

76

Boaz's obvious interest in Ruth) and does not want Ruth to run off with a young, unrelated and poor, man?

Naomi's newly found concern manifests itself in other ways as well. The sight of the grain sets her eyes bulging and prompts the demand to know where Ruth has been working. When Ruth reports that the man for whom she has been working is called Boaz that response prompts a sudden afterthought of inclusiveness: "And Naomi said to her [NIV: "She added"], 'The man is a relative of *ours*; he is one of *our* kinsman-redeemers" (2:20).[17] "Slowly," writes Trible, "the bitterness of an old woman is being transformed" (1978:179). The narrator, however, will not let her transform so easily, but immediately stresses "the national exclusion of Ruth by calling her a Moabite: 'And Ruth the Moabite said . . .'" (Trible 1978:179-80).[18] The juxtaposition of inclusion and exclusion, like the suddenness of Naomi's concern, suggests that Naomi's feelings about Ruth at this point are ambivalent still—she is uncomfortable about her and yet perceives her to be useful.

Naomi and Ruth's security: in search of a home

Naomi's ambivalence continues into Chapter 3 where she reveals to Ruth a plan. The plan, she tells Ruth, is for Ruth's future: "Should I not seek security for you that it may be well with you?" While Ruth's security is the subject of the proposal, Naomi knows well that her own security is now bound up with Ruth's. Indeed her language is again inclusive as she directs her daughter-in-law's attention to "*our* relative Boaz."

Her avowed concern for Ruth's long-term security, nevertheless, stands at odds with Ruth's short-term safety. Ruth is to bathe and dress up and to go down to the threshing floor in the middle of the night. The Song of Songs tells us of the risk a woman takes when she goes into the streets at night alone:

"When I sought him, I did not find him;
I called him, but he answered not.
The watchmen found me,
As they made their city rounds;
They struck me, they wounded me,

They stripped me of my robe,
Those watchmen of the walls" (5:6-7).

And discovered on the threshing floor, how might she be perceived by the men there?

"You have loved a harlot's hire
Upon every threshing floor,"

declaims Hosea (9:1), pointing us to one likely perception among men who have been drinking and who are inclined to molestation.[19] Yet Naomi sends Ruth off, again without a word of caution.

Naomi and the threshing floor

And what precisely does Naomi wish to happen on the threshing floor?

As is generally recognized, the course of action proposed and undertaken is heavily laden with sexual potential.[20] Ruth is directed to make herself attractive and go down to the threshing floor to "sleep" (*shakab*) with the man. The motif of the young woman introduced into the bed (so to speak) of an inebriated man, at night so that her identity goes unrecognized, brings strongly to mind not only the story of Lot and his daughters once more, but even more strikingly Laban's tricking of Jacob with Leah. Naomi tells Ruth explicitly to wait until Boaz has finished drinking. She never tells her to identify herself. It is the man who will say what to *do* (not speak!). Again the incognito motif points us to the Judah-Tamar story and Tamar's drastic ploy to force Judah to recognize her right to motherhood. She tricks him, of course, by "playing the harlot."

Why should Naomi set up such an arrangement? Allusion suggests that entrapment is the goal.[21] Sexual intercourse, if not pregnancy, will enforce either marriage or a pay-off. The man, remember (2:1), is a "man of substance" (or a "pillar of society," we might say[22]). He is also a relative (at least by marriage); all the more reason for him to wish to avoid a public scandal.

But why not approach Boaz directly? And why has Boaz not approached Ruth himself? (Our assumption here is that he is, indeed, interested in her—to that we return shortly.) What is wrong with Ruth as a prospective wife? We must leave aside for a moment that question as it applies to Boaz. But we can address it with regard to Naomi's perception.

What stands as a barrier between Ruth and marriage to Boaz, in Naomi's view? The answer must lie in the fact that Ruth is a Moabite woman. The text constantly offers us this point of view through persistent and carefully placed use of the epithet "Moabite woman."[23] Allusion to Lot's daughters and (perhaps) the women of Baal-peor compounds the sense of there being a problem in being a Moabite. And that perception fits well with what we have suggested earlier regarding Naomi's values. She understands the conventions only too well. A pillar of the community like Boaz cannot afford to pursue his interest in a Moabite woman in terms of marriage, unless under some kind of cloak or compulsion. Naomi decides to go for compulsion.

Ruth, of course, does not comply exactly with Naomi's scheme, but she gives her mother-in-law no indication at this point that she intends to vary the direction of the plan. As Ruth leaves, Naomi is assured that she will do what she has been told.

You must not arrive empty

On Ruth's return to Naomi after her night at the threshing floor,

> she told her all that the man had done for [to?] her, saying "These six measures of barley he has given me, for he said, 'You must not arrive empty [cf. 1:9] to your mother-in-law.'" (3:16-17)

Yet we know that those words purporting to come from Boaz are in fact Ruth's. Boaz had not mentioned Naomi. So why does she make up this message for Naomi? But once we notice this discrepancy and pause a moment to ponder it, we may likely notice something else—Ruth's silence about herself. For the narrator nowhere indicates that Ruth tells Naomi anything of what Ruth herself had done and said at the threshing floor, though that speech we know to have been crucial.[24] So why does Ruth keep silent over her own initiative?

One way of responding to both questions is to note that both the fabricated message and the focus on Boaz's action turn Ruth's reply into a reply about *Naomi*. Ruth fabricates an expression of Boaz' concern for Naomi in order to mirror what she knows to be Naomi's chief need—Naomi's personal security. It is Ruth's way of telling her, without forcing her to acknowledge that her future is in fact in her daughter-in-law's hands, that she is included in whatever "redemption" Boaz has in store for Ruth. In her account of the threshing floor story Ruth suppresses her own part in order to allow the story to stand as the story Naomi shaped. As Trible notes, Naomi had expected Boaz to tell *Ruth* what to do, not the other way round (1978:186). Ruth therefore lets the story stand that way. She allows Naomi to hold on to her sense of being in charge.

In other words, Ruth tells Naomi what she thinks Naomi wants, perhaps *needs* to hear. Our understanding, then, is that Ruth's report is determined by her sensitivity to Naomi's need for security and her emerging sense of self-worth.[25] At the same time Ruth cannot resist a small barb, perhaps hoping gently to push a reassured Naomi toward some small recognition of reality: "you must not arrive empty" she has Boaz saying, recalling, as she hands over the grain and the message of hope, Naomi's words at the gate of Bethlehem. Believe me, says Ruth to Naomi, I am not emptiness.[26]

A SON IS BORN TO NAOMI

"That Ruth may now find a husband," writes Trible on the conclusion of chapter 3, "satisfies Naomi's original concern." But the narrator never confirms such a concern; we hear about it only from the lips of Naomi. And if Ruth's welfare has been her sole interest, how odd that she should not be seen to celebrate that welfare. As Naomi earlier stood at the gate of Bethlehem, at the end of chapter 1, we were struck by her silence about Ruth. A similar silence marks out the very end of the book. Naomi is silent at marriage and birth, a silence that strikes the women of the city, so much so that they gently chide her by reminding her about the baby's mother, "your daughter-in-law, who loves you, who is more to you than seven sons." To which the mother-in-law responds without a word. She takes up the child. Her perception of the event is again mirrored through the speech of others: "a son is born to Naomi!" exclaim the women as she presses the child to her breasts.

At the heart of Naomi's impassioned speeches in chapter one had been her sense of deprivation. She had been left without husband or son. "Have I yet sons in my womb?" she had cried bitterly. "I am too old to have a husband!" "I went away full, and YHWH has brought me back empty!" Now as the story draws to a close she has, at last, a son. She is no longer empty. This, for her, would appear to be the story's resolution. Of Ruth, no mention.

SURROGATE MOTHERS

We have seen Leah and Tamar on the threshing floor with Ruth. Leah and Tamar come into view again in chapter 4, where the people and elders allude to them explicitly in the course of invoking a blessing upon Ruth and Boaz.

> "May YHWH grant that the woman coming into your house be like Rachel and Leah, who together built up the house of Israel," they say. "And may your house be like the house of Perez, whom Tamar bore to Judah, because of the seed that YHWH will give you from this young woman." (4:11-12)

Here the allusions would appear to carry a force that reaches beyond what the people and elders seem to have in mind as models of fruitfulness and architects of a male dynasty.[27] The message of the women, that "a son is born to Naomi," interprets Ruth to be a surrogate, which brings into focus other dimensions of the Rachel and Leah story, dimensions of jealousy and resentment that come when other women bear children for the barren. We are reminded also of Sarah and Hagar. Though establishing Naomi within the tradition, these narratives also undermine her triumph, for they reveal the solution of the surrogate to be an unsatisfactory one.

Savored thus, Naomi's silence is bittersweet. To be sure, she appears to have within her grasp the security of a son and a (surrogate) husband; Naomi is no longer "empty." But the image of the woman with the child at her breast is ambiguous—is she mother or only nurse? "A son is born to Naomi," say the women of the neighborhood, attempting to force the issue, sensing Naomi's need. But Naomi must know, as the reader knows, that despite its metaphoric appeal, this ascription of motherhood is only rhetoric. Any reality that it might have lies in the gift of her daughter-in-law—the daughter-in-law who is, in the words of the women, "better than seven sons."

So where does that leave Naomi? As she seeks to restore her hold on the patriarchal system, the narrative exposes the precariousness—and the irony—of her position. Whether she is willing to recognize it or not, she owes her restoration to a woman, to Ruth the Moabite woman, to Ruth the woman whose radical fidelity to another woman challenges the male-centered values that permeate both the story and Naomi's worldview. Calamity from the god of the patriarchy she has been quick to proclaim. Generosity from a wealthy man she is quick to praise. Grace from a foreign woman is perhaps beyond her comprehension. Little wonder that to the message, "your daughter-in-law who loves you is better than seven sons," her response is silence.

2

BOAZ
THE
MAN
OF
WORTH

A less than altruistic Naomi has emerged, a character caught and compromised by her cultural context and by the prejudices which spring from that context. What then of the character Boaz? Are there any such constraints on this "man of worth"?

Trible (1978) is relatively reticent about this "powerful male" who has to be goaded into action by the two women. Others are much less restrained. Campbell (1975), for example, cannot speak enough of the generosity, reliability and social responsibility of this hero. Yet if we have discovered a less magnanimous Naomi, what might we discover of Boaz, if we were, ungenerously, to peer behind his generosity, uncover his legs, so to speak, and confront his proclaimed worth with a counter-measure of value?

A "pillar of the community," is one way we have described him, loosely translating the label with which he is introduced by the narrator: *'ish gibbor hayil*, a man of substance, a man of worth (2:1). But we should be cautious about assuming in that value-laden label the unqualified approval of the narrator. The label may merely reflect the narrative community's perception of Boaz.[28] On the other hand it carries in it an invitation to the reader to evaluate, to measure worth. Boaz and "worth" are introduced together. What does Boaz see as "worth"? What does the community see? And might we, in conspiracy with the narrator, see something different?

We shape our discussion around three questions, three gaps in the text. First, why does Boaz marry Ruth? Second, why does he have to be pushed into taking an initiative over the marriage? Third, why does he have to have a public confrontation with the nearer redeemer in order to attain his goal?

WHY DOES BOAZ MARRY RUTH?

Boaz and Ruth: in the light of day

The first question might be rephrased: what is the nature of Boaz's interest in Ruth? Concern for her and Naomi's economic plight as widow and, in the case of Ruth, as foreigner, coupled with his sense of responsibility as a "redeemer," is the simple answer. Yet the text itself offers us something more complex.

Certainly he strides onto the scene as a man of faith. "YHWH be with you!" he says to the reapers in the field; "YHWH bless you!" they return (2:4). Likewise to Ruth he expresses a pious wish, "May YHWH reward you for what you have done . . ." Yet we have already had reason to pause over Naomi's similar words of generous piety. Is this anything more than the "right" thing to say? Does the invocation of blessing in fact help to preserve distance?

Moreover, as several critics have noticed, Boaz's speeches to Ruth in chapter 2, on the harvest field, are more than tinged with sexual overtones. Much is subliminal (cleave [dabaq], go to the vessels, drinking, eating)[29]; but not all. We have already mentioned the risk of the harvest field for a young unattached woman. Boaz's reiterated warnings about possible molestation by the young men (2:9, 15, 16; and cf. Naomi to Ruth, 2:22) are (to risk a pun) striking. His very first words to Ruth concern her need to stay in his field, to "cleave" to, and to "go after" (cf. 10) his young women, and to know that his young men are not going to "touch" her.[30]

84

Boaz knows all about her already. He knows, he tells her, all that she has done for Naomi "since the death of your husband" (not, we observe, "her [Naomi's] husband" as we might have expected if the focus were concern for Naomi). His immediate and abundant concern for her welfare is itself most touching if not, indeed, just a touch surprising. We might be forgiven if we begin to wonder whether his solicitousness in the matter of touching is to be construed, to put it anachronistically, as a classic case of a Freudian slip.[31]

Boaz and Ruth: in the dead of night

Such a reading may be confirmed, surprisingly perhaps, by the scene at the threshing floor. Surprising, since it is at the threshing floor that Boaz most obviously takes on the mantle of redeemer, acting with responsibility and generosity. Yet even here Boaz's speech cannot conceal that other perspective that sees Ruth in sexual terms, the object of his desire.[32]

The verse in question is 3:10, where the sexual longing slips out from under a paternalistic and pious blessing extolling the virtues of loyalty (*hesed*). "May you be blessed by YHWH, my daughter," breathes Boaz. "You have made this latter *hesed* even better than the former, in not going after the eligible young men (*bahurim*), whether poor or rich." For most commentators the "former *hesed*" is what she has shown to Naomi in coming with her to Bethlehem and supporting her through her gleaning.[33] On the "latter *hesed*" Campbell comments:

> the latter *hesed* . . . is her determination to play her part in keeping Elimelek's inheritance in the family and in making provision for two widows, not only for herself but for Naomi also. (1975:137)

But that interpretation lies a long way from the speech itself, which defines the measure of difference between the two acts of *hesed* in terms of not going after the young men. The immediate contrast is between the young men and Boaz, a contrast already obvious from chapter 2 (where young men connoted sexual interest) and here reestablished within the speech by Boaz's use of "my daughter" in addressing Ruth (vss. 10, 11). An obvious transformation of the clause "in not going after the young men" would be "in going after me!" Or as one ancient commentator puts it: "you desire an old man" (Rashi, in Beattie 1977:74). In other words, in keeping herself for Boaz and making a proposal of union with him Ruth has eclipsed her loyalty to Naomi. Here the condition for faithful action, therefore, unexpectedly centers around Boaz, his sexuality and his perception of Ruth's sexual availability.

That is not to say that this is all there is to Boaz's perceptions and actions. On the contrary, it is quite clear that Boaz is challenged by Ruth's powerful redeployment of his own pious words about the *kanaph* (wing or skirt)[34] of God (2:12) into subordinating his immediate sexual interest in Ruth to a more enduring interest which will incorporate, among other possible dimensions of the relationship, a serious concern for her social security.

It should be noted here that Naomi and Naomi's welfare is not part of this nocturnal discussion. Boaz responds to the request Ruth makes on her own behalf ("I will do all that you ask") and even in his talk of redemption,[35] his language suggests that Ruth is the sole object (second person singular feminine) of his concern.

Boaz and Ruth: at the dawn of a new day

What is veiled at this point is his concern for himself and his standing in the community. But his reputation is on his mind as we see the next morning when he is concerned that no one see the woman leave the threshing floor. Some commentators have even suggested that his gift of grain to Ruth is but a ploy. If anyone should see her, they could suppose that she had simply come to the threshing floor to buy food (Wojcik 1985:150; Hubbard 1988:222). Indeed, the question of Boaz's reputation may be as large a motivating force as his desire for Ruth. The analogy with the story of Lot and his daughters is suggestive. In that story the inebriated Lot unknowingly has sexual intercourse with his daughters. Our text implies that Boaz, too, has had a good bit to drink before retiring. When he comes to and finds a woman beside him and his "feet" exposed,[36] what does go through his mind? Might he not wonder if this woman has indeed had intercourse with him?[37] And what if she has conceived? The urgent expedition of Boaz's action and the particular avenue that it takes (weaving the announcement of marriage into a proposal about property),[38] may be due as much to his need to "redeem" his reputation as it is to rescue Ruth.

In the public light of the following day, Boaz's talk is all of redeeming land and continuing male lineage and property. But as the story draws to a close, the narrator allows Boaz's final action to speak for itself. For all his piety and generosity, for all his acclaimed responsible behavior, his desire for Ruth cannot be cloaked. His last, and most telling, move is to have sexual intercourse with "his woman" (4:13).

WHY SO RELUCTANT, BOAZ?

If Boaz so wishes to share Ruth's company (however we might construe that wish precisely), why does he make no initiative prior to Ruth's challenge on the threshing floor?[39] That is a question that has even bothered commentators who see a Boaz motivated only by concern for the needy, admiration for the valiant, a deep sense of duty, and a heartfelt piety—all of which might add up to something like loving loyalty and faithfulness. Perhaps, critics have ventured, since he already knew that there was a closer redeemer he knew that the responsibility lay with the other man; though even then his failure to press that person to do something positive about his responsibility tarnishes somewhat the hero's polished image.

Our own answer to this question has already been indicated in speaking of Ruth "the Moabite woman." As we have seen, both literary allusion and the careful deployment of epithets establish Ruth's Moabiteness as a crucial factor in the story. Her nationality is a powerful ingredient in the perception of Ruth by the community at large. That is to say, the conventional value attached to the label, "Moabite woman," especially in the context of marriage to a Bethlehemite man, is decidedly negative. Naomi, the woman of convention, knows well why Boaz does not move. An *'ish gibbor hayil*, a man of social standing, risks compromising his status if he openly courts a Moabite woman (cf. above, p. 79). Naomi decides to force the issue. Boaz, responding directly to Ruth, decides to use a cloak (the connection between cloak and assembly at the gate will become more apparent in a moment). This brings us to question three.[40]

WHY A PUBLIC CONFRONTATION?

Why does Boaz require a public confrontation with the nearer redeemer in order to attain his goal?

Why did he not just approach the "redeemer" (go'el) privately and on settlement of the matter then go through whatever public ceremony was required for the transferral of the redemption obligation? And why the confrontation? If (as appears clear whatever the interpretation of the legalities involved) Boaz was so confidant that the nearer go'el would refuse the deal, why did he have to trick him into first saying yes, and then no? Why not have made the complete proposal to him straight away? Commentators are heavy in their praise of Boaz's sagacity and tricky dealing, yet largely silent about why he indulges in any of this at all.[41] An appeal to dramatic tension is only half an answer, since it still leaves the plot without motive. No, it is important that this discussion between Boaz and near redeemer be competitive and produce a winner and that the confrontation take place in public.

Here we launch into the dreaded world of redemption and levirate marriage. Interpretations of this famous scene will continue to be debated while the Book of Ruth is read. Our own reading of the larger story, however, prompts the following understanding.

Redemption as a cloak

Boaz needs a cloak to cover his marriage to the Moabite woman. Ruth offers him the clue. In the most extraordinarily compromising position, she offers him a choice: "extend your *kanaph* over your maidservant—for you are a redeemer" (3:9). The language is highly ambivalent. It is (to simplify) either an invitation to have sex, or an appeal for marriage and security, or both.[42] The choice of interpretation is offered to Boaz. That is the risk that Ruth takes and a measure of her courage.

But the language is tilted in such a way as to offer direction also. Boaz is challenged to make good with action his earlier profession of pious well-wishing: "May YHWH recompense you for what you have done, and a full reward be given you by YHWH, the God of Israel, under whose *kenaphim* (wings) you have come to take refuge!" (2:12).

Ruth also names him *go'el*, "redeemer." What exactly she means by the term we cannot be sure.[43] She *may* be aware of the term as a technical one—a relative who saves property from passing out of the family[44]—but a sudden reference to property redemption seems out of place in the conversation. And, despite many commentators' assertion to the contrary, redemption as an institution has nothing to do with marriage, let alone levirate marriage. The relevant laws (in Leviticus 25 and 27 and Deuteronomy 25) are quite separate.[45] And, incidentally, though the question of levirate marriage is not raised on the threshing floor, Boaz has no obligation to offer marriage since levirate marriage is a matter for brothers who live together, and there is no good reason to suppose that Boaz is a brother of either Elimelech or Mahlon and certainly Boaz has not been living with either of the dead men.[46]

Of course, it is possible that Ruth *is* aware of the technical use of the term *go'el*. But, if so, her language may here be as deliberately slippery as in the preceding sentence. Her appeal may be from the technical label *go'el* to the broader meaning of "rescuer" which underlies the institution. And not just any rescue or rescuer—the verb is, of course, part of theological language and as such it readily finds its place in her speech alongside the image of the *kanaph* (read as "wing").

In short, an exegetical decision to understand Ruth's speech as implying some actual legal institution, obliging a (technical) *go'el* to practice a kind of levirate marriage, is an interpretive leap which it is not necessary to take.

But what Boaz makes of the remark is another matter. That he hears an urging to be a rescuer, after the manner of God, is possible, especially since he goes on to speak of "redeeming you." What, however, becomes very clear is that the remark prompts a train of thought concerning (technical) redemption. His reply, therefore, is couched in ambiguous language, allowing the possibility of (property) redemption to lurk alongside a more general meaning of help or rescue which could include marriage. What we must notice is that just as Ruth never explicitly asks for marriage, neither does the cautious Boaz explicitly promise it. Both the asking and the answering are in code.

But now Boaz has his cloak.

And so to the scene at the gate in Chapter 4.

Establishing the name of the dead

After Boaz's challenge to the nearer redeemer to redeem the field, and the redeemer's assent, comes the crux, verse 5.

> Then Boaz said: "The day you acquire the field from the hand of Naomi, I am also acquiring Ruth the Moabitess, the widow of the dead, in order to establish the name of the dead over his inheritance."

This translation differs from many of the standard English versions. The problem arises in the second instance of the verb "acquire" (which can also be translated "buy").[47] The consonantal text (the *kethib,* what is *written* in the Hebrew Masoretic Text), supposedly the more ancient witness, has a first person singular form. Later scribes, presumably uncertain of what was going on in this scene, recommended an altered reading and expressed this reading in the vocalizing of the text (the *qere,* what is *read*): "you are acquiring" instead of "I am acquiring." The alternative reading, the *qere,* has generally been followed in English translations.[48] Thus, the RSV translates the verse:

> Then Boaz said: "The day you buy the field from the hand of Naomi, you are also buying Ruth the Moabitess, the widow of the dead, in order to establish the name of the dead over his inheritance."

For various reasons we prefer to follow the consonantal text (as urged recently by Beattie and Sasson) and translate, "The day you acquire the field . . . I acquire Ruth." Reading the text this way maintains the distinction between the laws of redemption and levirate marriage in accordance with the laws in Leviticus and Deuteronomy. This reading also provides an important logical requirement of the plot. A piece of unexpected news is required to cause the near redeemer to back out of his commitment to acquire the field under the obligations of redemption. That news is Boaz's announcement of his marriage "in order to raise up the name of the dead to his inheritance." In other words, the near redeemer is suddenly confronted with the possibility that there could be a male heir to Mahlon and that the land for which he was about to expend good money could eventually revert to that heir.[49] That surprise only works if there is no expected connection, legal or moral, between the respective obligations of redeemer and levir—a point well made by Green (1982:58).[50]

As for Boaz, his act is *not* strictly an act of levirate marriage —that, as we have already noted, is a matter for certain brothers-in-law and he is not one. But Boaz has deliberately couched his announcement of marriage in the conventional terms of levirate marriage. Taking his cue from Ruth's association of marriage and redemption he has seen that the redemption of the field and his desired marriage can be presented in tandem, with his role as (official) *go'el* making his claim to (unofficial) levirate status so much the easier for the community to accept or indeed welcome.[51]

Making a virtue of necessity

Why the public confrontation? Because the essence of Boaz's operation here is public. He is in the business of effecting a dubious marriage in such a way as to make it a public triumph. He is a pillar of society and determined to remain that way. The name of the game is Public Relations and he is a master of it. The redeemer, therefore, is the luckless victim of a set-up—and in many ways this scene is the daytime counterpart of the night-time attempt at entrapment which was the subject of chapter 3.

Why confrontation? Because that way Boaz comes out a winner, and people love a winner. He is prepared to undertake the obligation to redeem, where Mr. So and So is not. All credit to Boaz. But much more than that, his is doubly a work of supererogation! For in addition he is prepared to act as *levir*—and not only that but to marry the Moabite woman into the bargain in order to do it! Why the gentilic, "Moabite woman," in verse 5, wonders Campbell (1975:160). Because Boaz is now making a virtue out of necessity![52]

All this is in the interests of establishing the name (fame and honor!) of the dead man over his inheritance (and notice that these *are* the terms in which the matter is put—and precisely *not* in terms of helping the poor and needy, especially the widow, which is what many critics are so anxious to see here[53]). The patriarchy loves it. What nobler end could one strive for, make sacrifice for? All hail to Boaz! All hail to the man who for sake of his brothers, living and dead, would marry a Moabite woman!

DEAD MEN'S NAMES AND A GENEALOGY

But the narrator has the final word.

First comes the mention of David, and the opportunity for us to cast Ruth, Naomi, and Boaz all to the winds and to decide that, despite its intricate plot and characterization, the purpose of the story is really designed to redound to the credit of the great king.[54] How wonderful for him that he should have had such splendid ancestry! Or, alternatively, how wonderful for her that she should have such a splendid descendent. Thus the story comes to expose our prejudice. For why must we deflect the woman's story toward the famous and powerful man, from the commoner to the king?[55]

Next comes the extended genealogy from Perez (the counterpart of Obed), the patriarchal history writ shorthand. And lo, it turns out that here too Mahlon and Elimelech are of no account. The line runs through Boaz to David. So much for raising up the name of the dead in his inheritance, that the name of the dead may not be cut off from among his brethren and from the gate of his place! "You are witnesses!" had proclaimed Boaz to all the people and elders at the gate, and "We are witnesses!" they had returned. And yet that generation of Bethlehemites could no more sustain into the future its witness to the names of the dead males than the generation of Joshua at Shechem could sustain its witness to the name of the living God (cf. Josh 24:22).

BOAZ'S FAITHFULNESS

So what is the measure of Boaz's faithfulness? His willingness to pay tribute to the patriarchy and subordinate all else to its rule? Viewed from one angle Boaz is as trapped by the patriarchy as Naomi, though he is trapped in privilege, she in dependency. Viewed from another, he is instrumental in mocking the system. He wishes to marry the Moabite woman and does so. His profession of commitment to the name of the dead is hollow. He cares no more for Mahlon and Elimelech than does the narrator. They are but weapons in his hand as he defeats one set of prejudices by wielding another. The measure of his faithfulness, then, surely lies somewhere else, somewhere in the offer of grain, and the spreading of a wing, in the exercise of *hesed,* for mixed reasons, in a compromised world.

Or is that too kind to Boaz?

3

RUTH
THE
MOABITE
WOMAN

Ruth, of all the main characters in this story, is by far the most enigmatic. Because her speech is less frequent and more cryptic than that of either Naomi or Boaz, the reader has more difficulty determining the extent of her awareness, defining her motivation, and pinpointing her tone. She has been described as a character of initiative—and indeed on a primary level she is—but one shouldn't overlook the fact that Ruth often moves in response to the other characters in the story. It is almost as though Ruth dances, sometimes in step, sometimes counter-stepping, between the two characters of Naomi and Boaz.

Ruth has also been identified as the theological center of the story. Indeed one recent author (Holbert) has found in this book the theological thesis "God is a Moabite widow."[56] And, perhaps, this is something the narrator is suggesting. But what of Ruth's perspective? How would she see herself? How would she describe her relation to the divine? Would she identify her movements as agency for some god? For those who see "God as a Moabite widow," the message becomes one of self-sacrificial love. Ruth follows through the "valley of the shadow." Ruth responds to the needs of others. Ruth gives with no thought of herself. The point preaches well, but carries a dangerous edge. The call to self-emptying has kept powerless people in their powerless places for centuries. For some the message is hardly liberating. Nor, we would argue, does the text constrain us to read this way. Rather, we suggest that the story sustains a more readily recognizable character, a character whose self is not totally eclipsed in its selflessness, a character whose motives, like most persons' motives, are mixed.

If we deem Ruth to be a realistic character, we must take a closer look at her and what she stands for in this story world. For homileticians she may be the center of the story, but what, for her, is the center of life? What forces motivate her to do what she does?

Ruth's character emerges in response to Naomi's crisis. She insists on returning to Bethlehem with her mother-in-law. Why is she so adamant? Her concern for Naomi seems clear. Even Naomi praises her *hesed* [1:8], implying that, whatever the circumstances now, the relationship between Ruth and Naomi has been a good one.

RUTH AND RELIGION

Also clear, some might argue, is her religious conviction. Having become part of an Israelite family, she recognizes their beliefs as a more true and excellent way. The trouble is that their way has seemingly led to nothing but trouble. Why should she attach herself to a family and a god who know nothing but death? What, we might wonder, is the nature of Ruth's "religious conviction"?

When we meet Naomi and Boaz, we meet people with the name of YHWH on their lips. YHWH is part of their worldview, though perceived somewhat differently—Boaz, the rich landowner, speaking in terms of reward, recompense and refuge, Naomi, the poor widow, in terms of calamity, affliction and violence. But what about Ruth? Is the name of God on her lips?

Yes, of course, we may answer, pointing to her famous "Don't push me to leave you" speech (1:16-17; usually cast in more genteel tone, as RSV: "Entreat me not . . ."). But consider that speech again. Its condition is Naomi's elaborate expression of frustration, morbidity and complaint against God, a complaint which sustains itself by fabricating a world of hypothetical sons, husbands, fertility. For these, in her world, are all that could possibly attract her daughters-in-law. She may as well be dead and so identifies herself with the dead of her family (1:8). Ruth responds in kind, in a brilliant piece of rhetoric which matches Naomi's concerns point by point and eventually confronts the vision of death underlying Naomi's speech and outdoes it. "Where you die, I die, and there will I be buried. [Then] YHWH may do the worst to me, I'll not be parted from you even by death!" Fickle Elimelech, Mahlon and Chilion, so quick to part, are deftly put in their place!

We are now, of course, in a world of hyperbole, on the edge of the absurd. Ruth mimics the older woman's rhetoric, indulges her grief and self-pity, but at the same time nudges her to confront real life. Ruth declares devotion to Naomi herself, not to her dead or hypothetical sons. Naomi does have someone to go with, she says, she does have a place to go to, she does have her own people, she does have a god, and someday she will die—but not today! Ruth uses hyperbole to attempt to crack Naomi's hypothetical world.

Ruth's speech does more, of course, than attempt to jar Naomi back to reality. Her willingness to change people and gods is also a response. Might she not perceive Naomi's discomfort with her Moabite daughters-in-law? And, since for Naomi, everything has religious roots, might Ruth not perceive that the discomfort with the two young women has religious roots as well? YHWH is punishing Naomi—that Naomi claims loudly enough—but for what? Is Moab the unspoken reason? Does Ruth therefore attempt to tame that fear by removing its theological roots? Understand the speech thus and we may hear her saying to Naomi: If you are worried that to continue association with a foreign woman with foreign gods is to invite further disaster, then don't worry, for I can fix that; I'll change people —your people will be my people!—and I'll change gods as well—your god will be my god!

Religious conversion serves another commitment: that of Ruth to her mother-in-law. The nature of this commitment requires some discussion.

RUTH AND NAOMI

Early stages

To understand Ruth's relationship to Naomi in the early stages of the story and her reasons for going with her, we must rely on the narrator's report as well as Ruth's speech. We notice in the scene the words "cleave/cling" (*dabaq*, vs. 14, used by the narrator) and "abandon/forsake" (*'azab*, vs. 16, used by Ruth). In this context of familial relationships, it is easy to pick up from the language overtones of familial/sexual usage from other passages, most notably, of course, Gen 2:24: "Therefore a man forsakes his father and his mother and cleaves to his woman/wife." Boaz's words about Ruth in chapter two also play with the same overtones: ". . . how you have forsaken your father and your mother and your native land and have come to a land you did not know before" (2:11). Such nuances suggest the image of Ruth as "husband" to Naomi and indeed, for much of the story, Ruth replaces husband and son as Naomi's caretaker.

More than familial imagery, however, surfaces in this vocabulary. "Cleave," "forsake" and also "turn [from] after" (*shub me'aharey*, vs. 16, used by Ruth; cf vs. 15, Naomi) are terms often used of relationship with YHWH and other gods. But Ruth, we notice, cleaves to and follows after Naomi, not Naomi's god. To be sure, she claims allegiance to Naomi's god. "Your god, my god," she declaims. But god in this speech ranks merely with lodging houses and burial plots. How easily Ruth changes her allegiance to Naomi's god! How easily, we could (ungallantly) wonder, might she change it again?—if circumstances so dictated. It is not commitment to the deity that concerns Ruth but commitment to Naomi.

And so Ruth leaves her native place and follows Naomi to a foreign land. Here many commentators see the first act of radical self-sacrifice and, indeed, her action is one of courage and commitment. But is Naomi the only reason Ruth is willing to go? What, exactly, is she leaving behind? We might draw analogies from modern interracial marriages. Often a marriage outside one's race (or in some cases, outside the "faith") means rejection by one's family and community. And if the "prodigal" is accepted back into the fold, the stigma of desertion remains. What are Ruth's opportunities in Moab? Who would want to marry a barren widow, much less one that had been living with a foreigner? And would she be known as the "Israelite-lover," the one too good for her own people? Or alternatively, the one who demeaned herself and her people?[57] In the end we might ask, what takes more courage, the staying or the leaving?

Why, then, does Ruth follow Naomi? The suggestion that Ruth may have reason to go to Bethlehem on her own account and take her chances with her husband's people, is not to diminish her commitment to Naomi. It is not inconceivable that Ruth is primarily looking out for herself, but we choose not to think her speech to be hollow. Rhetorical, certainly, but not empty. What, then, is the nature of Ruth's commitment? As far as the text is concerned, that is not defined. We suggest a loyal friendship that is not without mixed motives. Sacrificial love? Perhaps—but not a love that recklessly loses sight of the self.

Gleaning

Chapter 2 finds Ruth, the breadwinner, seeking the favor of any man who might let her glean in his fields, while Naomi remains at home. Ruth, having been sent forth by her mother-in-law without a word of warning about the dangers in the fields, spends a day working under the protection of the landowner Boaz.

Here, many readers find the second instance of self-sacrificing love: she works to feed her beloved mother-in-law. Yet Ruth must eat, too. And, when offered food at mealtime, the text expressly states that Ruth "ate *until she was satisfied*" (2:14). When she returns home, she gives Naomi "what food she had left over *after being satisfied*" (2:18). A curious detail to be repeated. That, no doubt, means a significant one. She shares with Naomi, clearly, but only after she has met her own needs first. Sacrificial love? Perhaps—but not self-emptying.

She returns home loaded with grain and mischief. We have seen how the sight of the grain prompts Naomi to suddenly include Ruth in her family. Ruth then teasingly reports to Naomi: "[The man] said to me, "You shall stay close to ('cleave

to') my young men . . ." though we know in fact that he
expressly cautioned her to "cleave to" his young wome...
Her words prod Naomi, for the first time, to express concern for
her, for her safety and her future: "Better, my daughter, that
you go out [and she noticeably does not use "cleave'] with the
young women lest you be molested." Ruth's strong hint of
possible separation (in order to cleave to unknown young men!)
forces Naomi to realize that the quality of her own future will
depend on that of Ruth. What we discover about Ruth from this
interchange is that sacrificial love cannot go long unnoticed.
Relationships must, on some level, be reciprocal. Ruth needs
recognition. Ruth needs Naomi's concern.

Ruth pulls acknowledgment from Naomi and, accordingly,
we are not surprised to find that in chapter three Naomi has
formulated a detailed plan to secure a future through her
daughter-in-law.

On the threshing floor

Naomi's scheme is dangerous and deceptive and we must
wonder why Ruth agrees to do it. Is she, like Naomi, willing to
do anything for the sake of security, anything to have a man?
Or is it her desire to "benefit not herself but Naomi's family"
that drives her (Hubbard 1988:66)? Is this her ultimate act of
self-sacrifice, that she offer her body for the sake of the older
woman's economic welfare (cf. Sakenfeld 1985:32 or Hubbard
1988:73)? Or is she merely naive and unaware of the sexual
implications of the plan?

An answer to the last question might be that ten years of
marriage weigh against the possibility of naivete. Answers to the
other questions rather depend upon how one understands
Ruth's character and the nature of her dance with and between
the characters of Naomi and Boaz. These relationships deserve
more attention.

As far as her compliance with Naomi goes, we do know that
she knows more than does Naomi. She has established a personal relationship with Boaz while Naomi has known him only
by proxy. At least one flirtatious interchange in Boaz's field

Ruth has kept to herself. Why? She surely knows that Naomi would be relieved to hear such a thing.

Ruth, we suggest, is biding her time. By waiting she gives Naomi time to sort out her feelings towards her, allowing Naomi to decide whether or not she wants Ruth to stay, to be part of the family (again). And indeed, no matter how selfish Naomi's motive for sending Ruth to the threshing floor, no matter how risky that plan, her proposal that Ruth go after Boaz *is* a way (if a somewhat left-handed way!) of saying that she wants her to remain in Bethlehem, to continue to be part of her life.

By waiting, moreover, Ruth nudges Naomi into taking some kind of action. Passive since arrival in Bethlehem, Naomi in chapter three at last makes a positive move. By not taking the initiative herself Ruth allows Naomi to feel needed, allows her to feel in charge, allows her to voice a reciprocal, even if half-truthful, concern.

Ruth allows Naomi to think that she is a party to Naomi's plan and, on the return, she tells Naomi no differently. The threshing floor scene is, as we shall see in a moment, rather different than Naomi had envisioned, but Ruth allows Naomi to think that her plan has succeeded. She lies about the grain she brings back home, insisting that Boaz has sent it to the older woman. In so doing, she conveys an implicit message that Boaz is acknowledging the plan's engineer and is pledging to respond to the situation in which he has found himself. By the same token, the lie assures Naomi that, whatever the outcome, she also will be taken care of. We know, of course, that Boaz on the threshing floor has not mentioned Naomi.[59] The pledge of care-taking is, in fact, Ruth's own. But Ruth, knowing Naomi's reliance upon men, couches the promise in a way that is sure to relieve Naomi's anxiety.

That Ruth is committed to Naomi, we see through her actions. She meets Naomi's loneliness with presence. But her speech is more complex. She voices her commitment in respons-es tailored to the older woman's view of herself, of her own needs, and of the constricted possibilities of her life. Her way, however, is not simply to follow Naomi's lead. She meets Naomi where she is, but also attempts to push her out of herself.

In the beginning Naomi elaborately declaims her lament as she argues for separation; Ruth matches her with passionate hyperbole as she insists on non-separation. Her speech shares Naomi's grief, but points her to the future. In chapter two Ruth leaves Naomi in her self-pitying silence, but only temporarily. She returns with symbols of life and hope and, with her pointed jest, she prods Naomi to look beyond the walls of her self-centered loneliness. Out in the fields, Naomi is forced to admit, both life and dangers await the companion she so ambivalently tolerates. In chapter three Ruth's silence allows Naomi to take the initiative; her laconic speech conveys submission, encouraging Naomi to think herself the manager of her daughter-in-law's affairs; and in the end her inventive explanation of the grain enables Naomi to to believe herself wanted and secure.

RUTH AND BOAZ

In the harvest field

Ruth's other partner in the dance is Boaz. She meets him in his field, conscious of the social hierarchy. She falls down in obeisance before him. She is a woman asking favor of a man. She is a widow asking permission to glean. But more than that, she is a foreigner asking to be treated like a native of the town. "Why have I found favor in your eyes, that you should take notice of me—me, a foreign woman?" is the first thing she says to Boaz. And she maintains the language of servility throughout the interchange.

On the other hand, it is clear that she is also picking up intimations of personal interest by Boaz beyond the formality of the landowner's response. His first concern is that she not be molested. He already knows of her marital status and what she has done for Naomi, and he enthusiastically approves of her. At the same time, his pious words and paternalistic "my daughter" maintain a proper distance between them.

By the end of the exchange Ruth herself is signalling more than a destitute foreigner's thanks to a gracious patron. "May I continue to find favor in your eyes" expresses "both a wish for future positive dealings and gratitude for Boaz's kindness"

(Hubbard 1988: 168). The phrase both concludes the conversation (Campbell 1975:100) and insinuates that she would like to continue this acquaintance (Hubbard 1988: 169; Sasson 1979: 52). "You've spoken kindly to your maidservant, though I am not one of your maidservants," she says with servility. Alternatively, her words to him have a flirtatious tinge: "You've spoken to the heart (*'al leb*) of your maidservant, and I [for my part] would not be [merely] like one of your maidservants." To "speak to the heart" is to speak tenderly, to woo; it is the language of the remorseful Shechem to Dinah (Gen 34:3), or the levite to his concubine (Judges 19:3), or YHWH to his bride-to-be Israel (Hos 2:14). Boaz has touched her heart and she tells him so.[60] If *his* language preserves distance between them, *hers* subtly hints at the possibility of closeness. But all the while she responds with appropriate deference, respecting the protocol. Yet she allows her words to do more than they say.

After the interchange Boaz invites her to join him at mealtime and afterwards, Ruth surely notices that her gleaning is much more productive than before. Kindness to a foreign widow? Perhaps—but not without a certain personal interest, a subtle music that Ruth has heard and to which she has stepped in time.

On the threshing floor

When Naomi comes up with her outrageous scheme in chapter three, Ruth assures her that she will do all that she says. But we soon learn that Ruth plays a variation on the theme. Granted, she goes to the threshing floor as she is told and she waits until the man finds a place to sleep. She uncovers his feet and lies down beside him. However, where Naomi had urged her to wait for the man to tell her what to do, Ruth confronts Boaz directly.

She puts her identity up front with all that it entails—she is a foreigner and she is "lower class" ("your maidservant"). But she puts it up front together with a challenge: Extend your *kanaph*, because you are a rescuer/redeemer. As with Naomi, Ruth allows Boaz freedom to make a choice. See her as but an ephemeral sexual object ("extend your penis"), or see her as a person in need ("spread your wing/skirt"), a person who offers an enduring relationship, in which sexuality will have its home. She "calls" him on his words of faith in chapter 2. It's fine to talk about the wings of YHWH, but how about something a little more tangible? You can afford to wait for YHWH to recompense, reward and offer refuge. I can't. How about putting your action where your fine words of faith are.[61] You talk of my *hesed*. Now let's see yours.

Not only does she pull his religiosity to the level of human interaction, she pulls it to the most basic level of human inter-action—sexual intercourse. His blessing (in ch. 2) allowed him to remain distant; she challenges him to cut through the dis-tance, to become as intimate as two people can be. She appeals to desire and closeness as a condition for faithfulness. And she extends to him her trust.

And so we return to the question, Why does Ruth take such a risk in this nocturnal visit to Boaz? We have seen how her relationship to Naomi has in part shaped her action. But when she speaks to Boaz on the threshing floor Naomi is not part of the conversation. We see her speaking and acting for herself and her own relationship to Boaz.[62] Boaz has spoken to her heart and she is responding.

Boaz's direct gift of grain, whatever his reason for giving it, carries a particular significance for Ruth. Before, he has provid-ed the grain indirectly, by allowing her to glean in his fields and by telling the harvesters to drop extra ears for her. This direct gift symbolizes for her that he is willing to overcome the dis-tance and to acknowledge the reality of his attraction to her. The grain suggests that he is offering her a more substantial relationship. She receives the "seed" from Boaz and passes it on to Naomi, assuring her that she, too, is the subject of Boaz's faithful action. Bearing the seed, she mediates between the two older people: she plays "wife" to Boaz, "husband" to Naomi.

RUTH AND YHWH

As the story draws to a close, the narrator reports (4:13) that YHWH gave Ruth conception. Would Ruth have agreed with this perspective? Babies don't come out of the blue. What YHWH "gives" has come through human interaction, through Ruth's initiative, Ruth's mediation, Ruth's loyalty, and Ruth's trust. Now human interaction includes sexual intercourse. "Intercourse between Ruth and Boaz is itself divine activity" (Trible 1978:193).

Hesed is something you practice, perhaps something you create, not something for which you wait to come from a distant god. "Your god, my god, anybody's god—what does it matter?" we might hear her saying. "Someone must be with you. Someone has to find food. Someone can rescue. And right now, what are *you* doing?"

In the end, however, the narrator's worldview supercedes Ruth's. For the narrator, the *hesed* that people must practice, the *hesed* that people create is indeed where God is found.

Almost exclusively absent as a character (4:13 is God's only direct appearance), God nevertheless pervades the story. Evoked in numerous blessings, God is a protector and a redeemer for the pious, the Boazes of Bethlehem. And that is important for people who must work out their own redemption. Because Boaz believes that God redeems, Ruth is able to challenge him to be a redeemer himself. She could not call him on his religious language if that language meant nothing to him. Consequently, the *hesed* that gets practiced in this case stems, at least in part, from the language of belief. Boaz's mundane piety turns out to be hardly mundane.

Nevertheless, it takes the outsider of uncertain religious conviction to precipitate, through action and words, Boaz's commitment to do *hesed*. And Ruth, as we have seen, offers us quite another perspective on the relationship between belief and *hesed*. It is her *hesed* that gives rise to religious language, both that of Naomi ("May YHWH deal *hesed* with you as you have dealt with the dead and with me") and that of her own ("Your people are my people; your god is my god"). Her impassioned speech of commitment to Naomi in chapter one, filled with its religious affirmation and divine oath, is the way in which she legitimates what she is about to do. And what she is about to do is probably the most loyal act Naomi will ever witness. And we believe her passion because we see her *hesed*.

In the book of Ruth, God is somewhere between belief and practice, the words and the actions, the relating of the human characters in this very human story world. God is not to be pinpointed, God's point of view cannot be determined, and God's providence is not to be equated with the speech or the action of any one of the characters. Nevertheless, God is here in this text. For the reader with ears to hear and eyes to see, God can be found somewhere in the mixed motives, somewhere in the complicated relationships, somewhere in the struggle for survival, anywhere there is redemption, however compromised.

CONCLUSION

We glimpse light in Ruth's story; yet the shadows fall across it again at the end. Ruth is eclipsed by a silent Naomi claiming a son and heir—and perhaps new strains in that relationship lie ahead. She disappears into the household of Boaz and a genealogy of her husband and son and the future king David closes the covers of her story. Who knows what conditions will shape her future, this woman of power? She has striven with the patriarchy and wrought security out of insecurity; yet her action has been all along conditioned by the system which set her story going and which remains firmly in place as it ends. If she has a way of jolting people to face a real world, so the story teller refuses to let us slip the knots of reality too easily.[63]

Perhaps she was recognized by Naomi as the real redeemer in this story. Perhaps not. Perhaps the gate of Boaz's people did come to consider her a woman of worth—like the woman of worth in Proverbs 31, a woman subservient, and thus valuable, to the patriarchy. Perhaps they only thought of her as Obed's (surrogate?) mother. Or perhaps, just perhaps, a few saw her as a woman of great strength and determination, a redeemer in her own right, deserving of her own story, a woman worth more than seven sons of Israel.

NOTES

BIBLIOGRAPHY

INDEXES

NOTES

NOTES TO INTRODUCTION

1. Hermann Gunkel once wrote:

". . . among the best known aesthetic creations of the Bible are those glorious *poetical narratives*, of marvellous insight and unique feeling for beauty of form, composed with truly classical sense of style, and therefore the delight of artists down through the ages and the theme of ever new creations, imitated again and again, in poetry and on canvas—narratives which bring the life of early days vividly before our eyes, a well of rejuvenescence for a civilization grown old, intelligible at sight to our children, beloved by them, and embodying for them lofty and eternal thoughts. Think of the force with which, in the Cain story, murder is set forth as the basal crime; the charm of the Joseph story, eloquent of fraternal envy and fraternal love, and full of faith in an overruling Providence; the attractiveness of the Ruth idyl, exhibiting a widow's love lasting beyond death and the grave; the magnificent solemnity of the Creation narrative; the wondrous story of Paradise, naive yet profound" (1928:20-21).

2. Quoted from Preminger and Greenstein 1986:3.

3. One point of dependence which will become obvious is Phyllis Trible's fine reading (1978)—a reading that is, like ours, both literary critical and feminist. It is a powerful and persuasive interpretation, one that has been very influential over the past decade. Yet our reading noticeably diverges from hers in various respects, not least on the character of Naomi. Like many other commentators, she finds Naomi to be a model of selflessness, whose dominant concern is for the welfare of her daughters-in-law. Naomi's support of Ruth, like Ruth's devotion to her, is exemplary. Ours is a less sanguine reading.

4. For an extensive account of how we read narrative in the Hebrew Bible, see Gunn and Fewell 1991. Other good starting points on narrative in the Hebrew Bible are Alter 1981, Berlin 1983, and Bar-Efrat 1989; fuller, but more difficult, is Sternberg 1985.

5. Sternberg (1985) takes many of these questions as his point of departure for an exploration of Hebrew Bible narrative.

6. Attention to point of view sharply differentiates our approach and that of Ronald Hals (1969) to the "theology" of the Book of Ruth.

He accumulates, and works from, direct and indirect references to God in the story without considering what differing perspectives form and inform this data.

7. See further, on the Hebrew Bible, Bar-Efrat 1984:47-92; cf. Bal 1985:85-91.

8. On the relation between genre and the construction of literary character, as well as a helpful discussion of other aspects of character, see Bal 1985:79-93.

9. One way of thinking about the coherence of characters is in terms of their "predictability"; cf. Bal 1985:82-85.

10. Thus Dale Patrick (1981) writes of characterization as the "evocation of presence" (involving the reader imaginatively entering into the thoughts and feelings of the character) and the "delineation of identity" (14). By the latter he means "the representation of a character with definite personal traits, coherently related to each other and consistently manifested in speech and deeds" (15).

James Phelan (1989:1-23) contrasts a mimetic approach to character, which views character as a representation of a possible person, with a structuralist view, which highlights the (artificial) nature of character as a literary construct, an accumulation of certain qualities, predicates, attached to certain proper names. While the latter view need not resolve apparently incompatible predicates, but merely observe their relationship, the former "tends toward the restrictive: it chooses among incompatible traits, it tries to build as precise a portrait of the character as possible" (8).

11. "The observation that 'acts, and even habits' may be inconsistent with a trait and that within a given personality there may inhere conflicting traits is absolutely vital to modern character theory," observes Seymour Chatman (1978:122-23) in the course of a very helpful discussion of character (107-138).

12. Cf. Wojcik's critique (1985:146-47) of Campbell's treatment of Ruth as a melodrama (Campbell 1975: 114-38) and Sasson's understanding of Ruth as modeled on a folktale (especially 1979:216).

13. On the notion of "filling gaps" in the text, see Sternberg 1985, especially chapter 6. This theory has been criticized by Bal on the grounds that it is "anachronistic and can in principle easily lead to bad criticism, including sexist interpretations" (1988:142; also 1987: 18-20). We fail to see the force of her argument; moreover, her charge could be equally levelled at most of the other interpretive strategies she espouses. On the other hand, we do not accept with Sternberg that the text will inexorably lead us (due to its "foolproof composition") to fill the gap in a such a way that the "true" meaning of the text ("the point of it all") will always emerge (cf. Sternberg 1985:50-51). On this latter point, see Fewell and Gunn 1991 and Gunn 1990.

14. For a discussion of feminist biblical criticism in recent times, see further Fewell 1987.

15. We pondered many ways in which to present our textual analysis. We wanted particularly to highlight point of view as an analytical tool. The idea of retelling the story focusing on different perspectives was the brainwave of Burke Long who, nevertheless, bears (of course) no responsibility for the result.

16. The ancient Jewish practise of *midrash aggadah* (meaning "interpretation of a biblical story") was expressed, for example, in the *targumim*, the Aramaic translations of the Hebrew scriptures between about 300 and 700 C.E. By carefully paraphrasing and augmenting with words, phrases and sometimes whole speeches, descriptions, and accounts of action, the translator attempted both to remain faithful to the Hebrew text and to restate the text in fresh ways, with a view to guiding the reader toward a particular interpretation. See further, Neusner 1987:26-30.

17. This way of describing how we teach and what we think is an important process in biblical exegesis comes from two colleagues at Perkins School of Theology, Richard Murray and W. A. J. Power, both of whom use such a strategy with theology students and laity.

NOTES TO PART I

1. The story of Tamar and Judah is found in Genesis 38. It lies at the beginning of the story of Joseph and his brothers, immediately following the brothers' disposal of him in the pit. Afterwards Joseph's story continues with the account of the young man in the house of Potiphar and his experience with Potiphar's wife.

2. Chezib is a proper noun of location. It is mentioned nowhere else in the Hebrew scriptures and is most likely a fictional place. There is a wordplay in its usage here. Coming from a root which means "to lie" or "to deceive," the place name not only foreshadows the deceptions yet to come in the story, but also suggests the nature of Judah's absence. The RSV follows the Septuagint [LXX], the ancient Greek translation, which reads "she [i.e., Judah's wife] was in Chezib."

3. See Alter's comment: "Interestingly, after we have been exposed to Jacob's extravagant procedures of mourning over the imagined death of one son, Judah's reaction to the actual death in quick sequence of two sons is passed over in complete silence: he is only reported delivering pragmatic instructions having to do with the next son in line. If this striking contrast underscores Jacob's excesses, it surely also makes us wonder whether there is a real lack of responsiveness in Judah, and thus indicates how parallel acts or situations are used to comment on each other in biblical narrative" (1981:7).

4. This custom has come to be called "levirate marriage" from the Latin *levir*, meaning "brother-in-law." For a description of this custom, see Deut 25:5-6: "If brothers dwell together, and one of them dies without a son, the wife of the dead one shall not become an outsider,

belonging to a stranger; her brother-in-law shall go in to her, and take her as his wife, and perform the duty of a husband's brother to her. And the first son whom she bears shall be established over the name of his dead brother, that his name may not be blotted out of Israel." This is not so much a legal requirement as a moral obligation. The brother can refuse, but at the risk of being publicly insulted by the sister-in-law (Deut 25:7-10).

5. We have borrowed this label from Maureen Duffy's poem of insight and poignancy, "Mother and the Girl" (1985:282-84). Our thanks to David Clines for sharing with us the poem.

6. On the story of Lot and his daughters, see Genesis 19 and our discussion of the use of literary allusions in interpreting the character of Naomi in Part II.

7. "Bethlehem" in Hebrew means "house of bread."

8. On the story of Baal-Peor, see Numbers 25 and our discussion below, Part II, on p. 72.

9. Several Hebrew texts bear witness to the belief that God controls the wombs of women. See, e.g., Gen 29:31-30:24; 1 Sam 1:19-20; Ruth 4:13.

10. Num 25:1-3; see above note 8.

11. A closer translation of this speech would be: "Go, return, each of you to the house of her mother. May YHWH deal *hesed* with you as you have dealt with the dead ones and with me. May YHWH grant that you find security [a home?], each in the house of her husband" (1:8-9). As one Perkins student, Gina Teel, has noticed, the language here does more than it says. Naomi is pointing the young women back to their own mothers and to homes with new husbands. On a more subtle level, the narrator allows the language to foreshadow the fact that Ruth will stay with the house of her "new" mother (mother-in-law) and will eventually find security in the house of her deceased husband, Mahlon.

12. It has been common in English versions to translate this passage (1:13) "It is exceedingly bitter to me for your sake." However, the most natural way to read the Hebrew is "It is much more bitter for me than for you" (cf., e.g., NEB; Campbell 1975:61; Trible 1978:170). The RSV and others have strained the language in order to depict a more altruistic Naomi. For a history of commentary on this passage, see Campbell 1975:70-71. See also below, p. 120 note 4.

13. On acceptance, see below, Part II, pp. 97-98.

14. In obvious contrast to the term "father's house," "mother's house" occurs but few times in the Hebrew Bible: Gen 24:28; Songs 3:4; 8:2. All are contexts of courtship, lovemaking, and marriage arrangements. See further, Campbell 1975:64-65. Though she cites these passages and Campbell's commentary, Trible seems to have missed this point when she asserts "[T]his phrase emphasizes the radical separation of these females from all males" (1978:169).

15. On Naomi's identification with the dead, see below, Part II, pp. 75.

16. On Naomi's treatment of Ruth at the gate, see below, Part II, pp. 75-76, and Trible 1978:174.

17. The Hebrew of 2:2 may be interpreted to mean that Ruth is asking permission to go: "May I go . . ." (NEB). But as in the English phrase "Let me go . . ." (RSV) there are more nuances possible, including the the polite informing that we translate here. Trible, too, takes the phrase to mean informing rather than asking. See Campbell 1985:91-92.

18. According to biblical law she should have had the right to glean, that is, take grain from the unmown edges of the field and from fallen ears or overlooked sheaves. Lev 19:9-10 and 23:22 specify that this right should be granted "the poor and the alien"; Deut 24:19-22 names "the alien, the fatherless, and the widow." As various commentators note, however, the reality may have been rather different so that the "right" may have been more like a "privilege" and very much in the gift of the owner. See further Hubbard 1988:136-37.

19. The Hebrew reads literally "her happening happened upon," i.e., "she chanced to happen upon the portion of the field belonging to Boaz."

20. This text is obscure and has several textual variants. We have adhered as much as possible to the traditional Hebrew text (Masoretic Text; see below, p. 123 note 15), though we have had to alter the punctuation somewhat. Our translation is as follows: ". . . and she came and she has stood [or "taken up a stand"] from this morning [literally, "from then, the morning"] until now. Her staying at home [literally "the house"] has been little." For the problems involved in this passage, see Campbell 1975:94-96 and cf. Hubbard 1988:149-152. As we do, Hubbard takes the word 'amad, "stand," in the well attested sense of "take up a stand" (and so wait; cf. 2 Sam 20:11, 12).

It makes sense in the context to see Ruth waiting, seeking permission to glean, especially since Boaz sees her immediately upon his arrival and addresses her without having to call her in from the field. It is possible that she must ask permission because she is a foreigner or it may be that the poor who glean usually do so after the harvest is finished. She is seeking to glean while the harvest is going on. Or, as Sasson has asserted, gleaning among the sheaves requires special permission from the owner (1979:47). Whatever the reason, Boaz's response suggests that she has in fact needed permission to glean. Hence, we believe our translation, which suggests that she has been standing waiting, to be more appropriate than one which has her working without resting (as, e.g., in the LXX or in the RSV).

21. The phrase "leave you alone" expresses the sexual overtones of the Hebrew verb ng' (2:9) which literally means "touch" but which in some contexts takes on overtones of violence or sexuality or both.

For a discussion of this and other indications of the menace of molestation faced by the foreign woman on this harvest field, see below, Part II, pp. 76-77.

22. The word *kanaph* has the basic meaning of "extremity." The term can refer to a wing (e.g., Isa 10:14; Exod 19:4), the skirt of a garment (e.g., 1 Sam 15:27; 24:5ff), or euphemistically to male genitals (Deut 22:30 [Heb 23:1]; 27:20). See below, p. 128 note 42.

23. The last clause in Ruth's speech in 2:13 is wonderfully ambiguous in Hebrew. It could be translated literally"[you have spoken to the heart of your maidservant] and I am not [even] as one of your maidservants" or "but I would not be [merely] as one of your maidservants." More idiomatically, eliminating the ambiguity: "though I am not so much as one of your maidservants" (Jewish Publication Society Tanakh) or "but I do not want to be like one of your maidservants" (cf. Jouon 1953:57).

The difference is between an expression of servile humility and one insinuating a desire for preferment. Auld comments aptly: "She [Ruth] has termed herself his 'maidservant' and then discreetly notes that this may not be so. The words cover two meanings and doubtless both are intended! She could be covering possible presumption and she could already be open to higher preferment—not *even* a servant, or not *just* a servant" (1984:269). Compare the NEB: "may I ask you as a favour not to treat me only as one of your slave-girls?" It footnotes as an alternative: "If you please, treat me as one of your slave-girls." The NEB's successor, the Revised English Bible, unfortunately revises away all ambiguity.

24. The text says that her grain was "like (or as) an ephah" (2:17). An ephah is variously thought to have weighed between 29 and 47.5 pounds (or about 13 to 21.16 kg). Some commentators take the *ke* ("like") as meaning "about." Another proposal is that it means "exactly." We would suggest that it may be idiomatic, in a hyperbole, as in English "the grain weighed a ton" or in the British English colloquialism "she collected like a ton." In any case, Campbell's comment deserves repeating:"The amount Ruth carried home was rather impressive for a gleaner, but we are not called upon to add to her list of virtues that she was as strong as an ox" (1975:104).

25. A redeemer (Hebrew: *go'el*) is a male relative who can be called upon to rescue property of a poor relative from going out of the family (see Lev 25:25-34) or to prevent a poor relative from being sold into slavery (see Lev 25:35-55). Supposedly, the closer the relative, the more obligated the redeemer. Because the redeemer is a close kinsman, the term is sometimes translated "nearest kin," "next of kin," "near kinsman" (see, e.g., RSV Ruth 2:20; 3:9, 12; 4:1, 3, 6, 8). The term is sometimes used to refer to a close relative whether that relative ever functioned as a redeemer or not. The metaphor, God as redeemer, probably stems from the word's social usage, though in theological

usage, the idea of payment recedes and the force of the word seems to be more like "rescuer."

26. On Ruth's use of the gender specific "young men" in 2:21, see below, Part II, pp. 76-77 and especially p. 123 note 15.

27. The season is not precisely winter, but it is a period of time when there is nothing to be harvested and people must depend upon the food they have in storage. The yearly climate consists of a dry, warm season (summer) and a wet, cool season (winter) with virtually no intermediate seasons. See Hopkins 1985:79-81.

28. The narrator describes Boaz as an *'ish gibbor hayil*, which could be translated literally "a mighty man of strength." The meaning of *hayil* depends upon its context: it can mean, e.g., valor in a military context. Here it denotes "substance" which could be political importance, social standing ("reputation"), material worth ("wealth") or even moral worth, or all of these.

Boaz is also the name of one of the two bronze pillars, Jachin and Boaz, that stood at the entrance to Solomon's temple (1 Kings 7:21; 2 Chron 3:15-17). While the meaning of Jachin is "he establishes," the meaning of Boaz is less certain, though probably something similar. Perhaps it was originally "in him is strength," or "in the strength of [Yahweh]," though in its present form neither meaning is grammatically obvious. See further the discussion in Campbell 1975:90-91. Whatever the precise meaning of the name, the fact that it is the name of the temple pillar must surely have prompted many readers, ancient and modern, to see a connection between the man of great standing and the pillar of the temple. Hence our own wordplay: Boaz is a "pillar of the community."

29. On precipitation in Palestine and its effect on agricultural practices, see Hopkins 1985:84-91.

30. Boaz's marital status is not defined in the text, but we might assume that any immediate family would have been mentioned.

31. "At harvest time labor supply appears to be more decisive than the availability of land resources in determining the extent of production" (Hopkins 1985:226; see also 233).

32. Nowhere does the text offer any clue as to whether Ruth was considered physically attractive or not, though a centuries old (mostly male) interpretive tradition has no doubts about the matter. Thus, for example: "We see the young Moabitess with her strange beauty and gentleness winning all hearts" (Manning 1890:45). Or from some ancient Jewish commentary which Beattie (1977:191-92) has conveniently summarized: "She was forty years old at the time of the story [Ruth Rabbah VI 2] but still very beautiful. To Boaz's words 'that you have not gone after young men, whether poor or rich' (iii 10), ibn Ezra adds 'for all love you on account of your beauty' and, commenting on ii 11, Salmon points out that 'Boaz knew that all the men, every one of them longed to marry her'. The ultimate tribute to Ruth's physical

attractiveness is to be found in R. Johanan's interpretation of *wyqr*
mqrh [literally, "and her chance chanced upon"] (ii 3)—'everyone
who saw her ejaculated semen' (*mryq qry*)." Our readers should
understand that we join the tradition with no little misgiving!

33. Some commentators understand this question—"Whose
young woman is this?" (2:5)—to mean that Boaz does not know Ruth,
(e.g., Trible 1978:178). His next speech, however, suggests otherwise.
Furthermore, there is some debate over the nature of the question.
Some argue that its indirection—"Whose is she?" rather than "Who is
she?" is simply an ancient oriental convention; perhaps it was considered impolite (or even suspicious) for a man to express a direct interest
in a woman of another family (cf. Gray 1967:391; Hubbard 1988:146).
If so, the fundamental reason is likely to be rooted in the notion of
women as men's possessions. Trible, therefore, has a strong point
when she remarks: "Truly a patriarchal question" (1978:176). As she
goes on to observe, the overseer cannot answer the question directly
because Ruth has no man ("lord"). Hence the overseer moves a
second level of "belonging": he identifies her by her nationality and
the fact that she had come with Naomi from Moab. Notice how Moab
dominates his identification. Notice also that he does not call her by
her own name, though he does name Naomi. It is as though Ruth is no
person in her own right.

34. The reference to Gen 12:1-5 has long been recognized (e.g..
Salmon ben Yeroham's tenth century commentary; see Beattie 1977:
66). Trible discusses this allusion, noting that ". . . Boaz adds an
ingredient—which was both clearly present in the call of Abraham and
noticeably absent in the choice of Ruth—the ingredient of divine
blessing . . . Boaz's language envelops Ruth within the Abrahamic
paradigm of the foreigner who breaks with the past and receives the
promise of blessing for the future. But differences remain. Ruth herself
chose to abandon the past without call or blessing. The divine blessing
extended to her now comes not directly from God but through a
human being" (1978:177, see also 173).

35. The Hebrew phrase is literally "to speak to the heart" (2:13).
It is strongly affective language, implying an effect upon the one
spoken to. See further below, Part II, pp. 101-102 and 132 note 60.

36. The question is, *whose* kindness does she mean? Boaz's or
YHWH's? The ambiguity of the English here reflects that of the Hebrew
text.

37. See further, Niditch 1979.

38. The sheepshearing was a time for more than just shearing
sheep. There was usually feasting and general festivity. In biblical
narrative it is also the occasion for some dramatic incidents: Rachel
steals her father's household gods (Genesis 31); David is prevented by
Abigail from murdering Nabal and his household (1 Samuel 25);
Abasalom has his brother, Amnon, murdered (2 Samuel 13).

39. There are various wordplays involved in this list (Gen 38:18), the most striking being generated by the word *matteh*, which means "staff" but which can also mean "tribe," and which most probably could also be used as a sexual euphemism.

40. This story is found in Genesis 29.

41. This threshing floor is probably communally owned and situated outside the town. Since transportation is inefficient, the floor may be imagined as being not too far from the grain-producing fields. See the discussion by Hopkins 1985:225-226 and compare Campbell 1975:117-119.

At this time of the year, perhaps June, the daytime temperature would be high (the mean daily temperature about 25°C [77°F]), relieved in the mid-afternoon by a sea breeze from the West. This wind would be used in the winnowing (Hopkins 1985:81), especially when it was "steady but not boisterous in the evening and early morning" (Gray 1967:417).

The end of harvest was a time for festivities (Sasson 1979:65; Auld 1984:272). In this respect it was probably rather like the sheepshearing (see above, p. 116 note 38). It is widely thought that Boaz was sleeping by the grain pile to protect it (see, e.g., Manning 1890:46; Gray 1967:417). Sasson, however, argues against this view, observing that "Boaz was far too important a man to keep watch through the night; he most certainly could have asked on of his many 'men' to assume such a charge. Additionally, it would certainly have been strange for any man to prepare for an all-night vigil by copiously consuming food and drink" (1979:65). He thinks, instead, that Boaz's act is connected with some festive ceremony. Whatever the case, the passage may readily be interpreted to mean that enough food and wine was consumed to render Boaz, and no doubt others, far from sober ("his heart was good/merry" [3:7]; cf. Nabal in 1 Sam 25:36, Amnon in 2 Sam 13:28—both at sheepshearing feasts—or Ahasuerus in Esther 1:10). To stay the night at the threshing floor would save an unwanted and, in the circumstances, probably hazardous walk back to town. The summer night would be pleasant, and for the owner, as Gray notes, there would be the advantage of being on hand to see that the work resumed in timely fashion with the early morning breeze (1967:417).

42. "Stay out of sight until after the man has finished eating and drinking . . . You don't have to say anything." These phrases render the Hebrew clause which can be translated literally: "do not be known by the man [until he has finished eating and drinking]." Among the various nuances of the Hebrew word "to know" (*yada'*) is one that cannot be missed in a context of such seductive potential as this, namely "to have sexual intercourse with." See, e.g., Campbell 1975: 131-132); Auld 1984:272.

43. For the phrases "gate of my people" and "woman of great determination," see the discussion of this sentence (3:11), below, p. 127 note 40.

44. A medieval rabbinic commentator writes, "He was quick to rise for he said, 'There is no honour for me in its being known that the woman came to the threshing-floor'" (Beattie 1977:127).

45. "He filled her lap with grain" is our free interpretation of the Hebrew text (3:15) which leaves the specifics unclear. As various commentators have noticed, the giving and receiving of the grain here is wonderfully symbolic of the promise of fertility underlying the exchange between Boaz and Ruth in this scene at the threshing floor.

Green (1982:63-64), e.g., sees the connection between the grain/seed and semen as an extension of the root symbol, the field as a representation of the woman. We try to render that symbolism a little more transparent. While the term "lap" does not appear literally in the Hebrew neither does the term "back" as the NEB would have it, interpreting Ruth as Boaz's beast of burden ("and he lifted [the filled cloak] upon her back"). The word *mitpahat*, translated often as "mantle" or "cloak," we term "apron." Actually the precise meaning of the word is unknown, except that it seems to be a woman's garment of some kind. Thus Green suggests "shawl" (63). The word occurs elsewhere only in Isa 3:22. The LXX translates it *perizoma*, which means a girdle or apron (e.g. a cook's apron).

Perhaps word-play is at work here. The related verb *tph*, seems to mean "extend," "spread," "stetch out," but also possibly "give birth" (Lam 2:22 — see e.g., NEB, NASB and JPS TANAKH; others translate "dandle"). Additionally (or alternatively) there is likely a wordplay on *mishpahah*, "clan," already in 2:13 probably the subject of a wordplay with *shiph-hah*, "maidservant" (cf. Campbell 1975:101).

46. The gate was also commonly the scene of legal judgments and transactions, which is also what Boaz has in mind in choosing this location for his encounter with the near redeemer. He is wanting a very public and official setting, for reasons that will shortly became apparent.

47. This is the first we have heard of this land and its sudden introduction into the story (4:3) has been a cause of puzzlement to generations of commentators. Why has it not been mentioned before? Why has it been of no apparent benefit to Naomi up until this point, so that Ruth has been forced to glean for food? When did Boaz learn from Naomi about the sale? How is it that Naomi has the right to dispose of the land, since widows did not normally inherit property (though there is an notable exception related of the daughters of Zelophehad, Num 27:1-11; 36:1-12)? Should it not have passed to Elimelech's sons and through them to a male relative? For discussion, but not solution, of these and related problems, see further Campbell 1975:157-58 and Hubbard 1988:52-56.

Two points we would make. First, as others have suggested, we take the text's silence on the point to suggest that Boaz has not in fact consulted Naomi about the sale. Confident that he can obtain right of redemption (though, as we shall see, that is not his primary aim here) he knows that the only difference the change of redemption rights will make to Naomi will be that if she does decide to dispose of her interest in the field she will have a sympathetic purchaser with whom to deal. Second, when Hubbard comments, "One might assume that [Naomi] needed the money, but "the text seems more concerned with inheritance matters than with Naomi's poverty" (1988:55), we would observe that such concern is strictly a matter of point of view. It is not Naomi or "the text" that is concerned with inheritance but the men at the gate whose interest Boaz shrewdly addresses. There is no reason to suppose that either Naomi or Ruth were not primarily concerned about their own poverty. On the contrary, the desperate measures they resort to in chapter 3 suggest that destitution was a powerful motivating force for both of them. And on a more contemporary note, as several of our students have observed, landowning and destitution need not be entirely incompatible conditions, as Scarlett O'Hara discovered in *Gone with the Wind*.

48. On labor supply, rather than the availability of land, as the crucial determinant of production, see above, p. 115 note 31.

49. Here we make an important choice regarding how we read the Hebrew at 4:5 where the MT offers two options. We follow the option which leads to the translation "Then Boaz said: 'The day you acquire the field from the hand of Naomi, I am also acquiring Ruth the Moabitess, the widow of the dead, in order to restore the name of the dead to his inheritance.'" This translation differs from many of the standard English versions, as, e.g., the RSV: "The day you buy the field from the hand of Naomi, *you* are also *buying* Ruth the Moabitess . . . " (our italics). The first difference is that we understand Boaz to be declaring his own intention to marry Ruth when Mr So-and-So redeems the field, whereas the RSV understands Boaz to be stipulating that Mr So-and-So must marry her. The second difference is between the translations "acquire" or "buy" for the verb *qanah*. Both are common meanings of this verb. For discussion of the issues involved, see below, Part II, pp. 90-91 and notes.

50. The speaker is refering to the custom of levirate marriage (see above, p. 111 note 4). He has inferred that this is what Boaz has in mind from the language Boaz has used, literally, "to raise up the name of the dead man over his inheritance." Compare the law in Deuteronomy 25 where the duty of the *levir* is said to be to enable his dead brother's wife to bear a son who "shall rise up over the name of his brother, the dead man, that his name may not be blotted out of Israel" (v. 6) and "to raise up the name of his brother in Israel" (v. 7).

51. According to Deuteronomy 25, if a brother-in-law declines to perform levirate marriage the widow may publicly pull off the man's sandal, spit in his face, and say, "So shall it be done to the man who does not build up his brother's house" (vv. 7-10). Here the sandal's function differs but it's mention prompts the reader to recall the Deuteronomy passage and its association with levirate marriage.

52. The phrase "who built the house of Israel" is another that may remind a reader of the law regarding levirate marriage: "So shall it be done to the man who does not *build his brother's house*" (Deut 25:9).

53. On Hagar and Sarah, see Genesis 16 and 21; on Bilhah and Rachel, see Genesis 29-30.

54. Chapter 4 has been dominated by men, men's voices, men's concerns, men's names. "But now the women redeem this male theme. They identify the child as the son of Naomi rather than of Elimelech. They perceive this infant as restoring life to the living rather than restoring a name to the dead" (Trible 1978:194).

NOTES TO PART II

1. When Genesis 19 is read through a gender lens, the depiction of Moab is more ambivalent. The daughters of Lot, recently offered to a rapacious crowd, their husbands-to-be lost in the devastation of their home and their mother in their flight from Sodom, perceive that they and their father are the only ones left in the world. Their subsequent deception of their father might then be seen as a heroic, ingenious attempt to save the species.

2. Hubbard, too, has picked up these overtones: "to seek refuge in Moab—Israel's enemy throughout history—was both shameful and dangerous" (1988:87).

3. An alternative translation would be "womb," though that is more normally in Hebrew *beten* or *rehem*. The word here, *me'ay* (from *me'im*), though usually a more general term for abdomen, does occur in contexts where "womb" or even "female genitals" would be an appropriate translation (e.g. Song of Songs 5:4). (See further Campbell 1975:66-67; Trible 1978:197 note 11; Sasson 1979:24.) Campbell observes that *me'im* is "sometimes the location for what we might call 'gut-feelings.'" In that case the term would be doing double duty here: it is both "womb" and a seat of emotions. That is why we we have preferred "belly." Ironically, while Naomi denies (literally) having sons in her "guts" she obviously cannot (metaphorically) get sons out of her system. Cf. Hubbard 1988:109.

4. "For it is more bitter for me than for you" is the most obvious way of construing the Hebrew here, though many English versions, no doubt to preserve a more altruistic Naomi, translate, "for it is exceedingly bitter to me for your sake" (so RSV). One rabbinic source ex-

pounds it thus: "It is very bitter for me, more than for you, for it is possible for you to be married to new husbands, but since my husband and my sons are dead it is not possible for them to return again, and I am too old, also, to be married (again)." Thus, continues the commentator, the further clause, "for the hand of God has gone out against me" means that "it has gone out against me and not against you" (Beattie 1977: 116). See also above, p. 112 note 12.

5. Hubbard sees her speech in vv. 11-13 similarly: "Ostensibly, the soliloquy is a passionate plea addressed to the women. In fact, however, it amounts to a lament accusing God of cruelly botching up her life. Its effect is to affirm his direct involvement in the story and hence his accountability for her awful situation. Further, it offers a peek both at Naomi's inner pain and her own interpretation of her tragic circumstances" (1988:108). On the other hand, in denying that Naomi (like Job) has done something to deserve her plight (127), Hubbard does not explore Naomi's own perspective. We suggest below that Naomi herself may be ambivalent about whether or not she has "sinned."

6. In line with this interpretation, the Targum, the ancient Aramaic paraphrase, saw the marriages to the Moabites as the cause of the deaths: "And because they had transgressed the edict of the Memra of the Lord by marrying into foreign nations, their days were cut short. And both Machlon and Chilion also died on unclean soil" (Levine 1973:20). Or as an anonymous Rabbi puts it: "*And Elimelech died.* This is said to teach you that if he had remained alive he would not have allowed his sons to marry foreign women" (Beattie 1977:114-15). And again: "*Go back, my daughters. Why would you go with me?* If it is to marry men of my people that you are returning with me, there is no man in Israel who will leave the daughters of Israel and marry you . . ." (116).

Other ancient Jewish commentators saw reason for guilt in the family's moving from Bethlehem to Moab: "Why, then, were they punished? Because they left Palestine for a foreign country; for it is written, And all the city was astir concerning them, and the women said: 'Is this Naomi?' What [is meant by] 'Is this Naomi?'—R. Isaac said: They said, 'Did you see what befell Naomi who left Palestine for a foreign country?'" (Baba Bathra 91a).

7. See Alter's reading of the relationship of Genesis 38 to Genesis 37 (1981:3-12).

8. We follow the LXX here. The alternative vocalization of this phrase yields the meaning "YHWH has testified against me" (so the MT; see Campbell 1975:77 for an argument in favor of the MT). The ambiguity of the phrase expresses the ambiguity of Naomi's understanding of her predicament. To be afflicted by YHWH suggests that she is an innocent victim. That YHWH has testified against her indicates that her calamity has been some kind of just punishment.

9. See further Campbell (1975:70-71 and 76-77) for a discussion of the language used in vv. 11-13 and 20-21, especially the term Shaddai ("Almighty") which occurs typically in Job and Psalms in contexts of complaint and lament.

10. Trible is also struck by this oversight and suggests that it is because the elderly widow is "overpowered" by her sense of divinely inspired calamity (1978:174). In a wonderful little book we came across as our book was going to press, Colleen Ivey Hartsoe has Ruth write in a letter to Orpah,

> "I felt the shadow of rejection pass over me . . . How could she say she was empty; how could she say disaster was on her? I knew then she did not love me the way I loved her. I wondered why she had let me come with her" (1981:32).

11. Recognition of the unattached young foreign woman's vulnerability to sexual assault in these harvest fields is widespread in readings of Ruth. A 12th century C.E. rabbinic commentator observes: "After [Boaz] said to her, 'Do not go to glean in another field,' what need was there for him to say, 'and do not go away from here'? The texts says this because he said to her, 'Do not go to glean in another field so that you will not be molested in another field, for it is a disgraceful and abhorrent thing for a woman to be molested by young men.' In case she should think, 'Even here Boaz's men may molest me,' it is said 'Thus you shall stay close to my young women and I have commanded my young men not to touch you'" (Beattie 1977: 122). Another traditional Jewish source has Ruth later informing Boaz that since she has been in Bethlehem she has been "constantly menaced by the dissolute young men around" (Ginzberg 1913:34).

Another reteller of the story (Spence 1924, using dramatic form) has Ruth verbally abused as a "harlot of Moab" and be subject to "personal violence" from other gleaners. She is rescued by a character, Tubal, only to be accosted by him in turn: "Ho! Pretty one, didst think I was helpful / To thee without reward? Come! Give a kiss! / Those looks of thine could buy thee half the harvest . . . ." (22-25).

Some critics, however, cannot imagine that such behavior could take place in the fields of Bethlehem and discount the sexual threat. So Sasson (1979:50), arguing by ridicule, finds it "unlikely that in the midst of the harvest, Ruth was to be pounced upon by crazed Bethlehemites," and speaks instead of her risking being "shooed away." Hubbard (1988:159, 177, 191-92), too, takes pains to censor the sexual from the scene, which he does by defining the key verbs—ng' (v. 9), klm (v. 15), g'r (v. 16) and pg' (v. 22)—all in terms of g'r, the word which most clearly indicates verbal rather than physical assault and which, when taken out of its present context, least obviously connotes sexual abuse. While it seems reasonable to interpret the aggression as stemming from others guarding their own preserve such an interpretation does not explain the careful distinctions made between the threat of the males and and the protection of the females.

Hubbard does acknowledge, however, a factor that is important in our reading, namely the probability that racial/ethnic prejudice renders her additionally a target (1988:137).

12. The verb ng' (2:9; literally "touch") is commonly used in contexts where it takes on a connotation of violence (e.g. Gen 26:29; Gen 32:26, 33; Josh 9:19). When used in the context of male-female relationships, it carries sexual connotations (e.g. Gen 20:6; Prov 6:29). Both connotations are probably present in Gen 26:11 and so, too, here. So the RSV, the JPS TANAKH, and other versions appropriately translate "molest" here.

13. Alternatively, "leave it," that is, leave whatever is pulled out of the bundles.

14. In the causative form the verb klm (2:15) means "to put to shame," "humiliate," "disgrace," "dishonor" (and is so understood by the LXX). Sexual harassment offers the most obvious source of such "shaming." This understanding probably underlies the JPS TANAKH translation, "without interference." Translations such as "reproach" (RSV), "find fault with" (Revised English Bible [REB]) or "deter" (Campbell 1975:103) unacceptably weaken the verb and censor the notion of (sexual) shame.

The verb g'r (2:16), often translated "rebuke," is used of verbal violence (thus, e.g., God will so speak to the threatening nations who will then flee, Isa 17:13; cf. 54:9). Hence we use the term "harass."

15. Throughout chapter 2, the reference to the workers and servants of Boaz have been gender-specific, either "young men" (ne'arim) or "young women" (ne'arot). As far as the Masoretic text (see below) and LXX[B] are concerned, Ruth's reference in 2:22 is also gender-specific: ne'arim, "young men." Sensitivity to the significance of these gender shifts in the context of the threat of molestation has a long history; see, e.g., the rabbinic commentary (c. 12th century C.E.) quoted in Beattie 1977:122. Many English translations (KJV and NEB are notable exceptions), however, miss or fail to understand the specific masculine gender in 2:22. This is a misunderstanding which obviously also has a long tradition — the Old Latin and some LXX manuscripts change the form to feminine to align Ruth's speech with Naomi's (see Campbell 1975:107). But Auld has nicely observed the storyteller's finesse here: "There is even some subtle mischief between older and younger generations concerning Ruth's relations with Boaz's 'lads' and 'lasses' . . . Ruth is quite clear that she can look after herself in mixed company" (1984:267).

The Masoretic Text (MT) was the Hebrew text that was "handed over" or "handed down" from generation to generation, the standard text of Judaism and some streams of Christianity. (Masor means "to hand over.") It is extant in complete manuscripts from about the tenth century C.E. One of the contributions of the scholars who preserved this tradition was to develop a system of representing the vowels in the text which was originally written with consonants only. In some places where the scribes wished to preserve two possible ways of reading the text, they combined the consonants of one word (the *kethib*, what is *written*) with the vowels of another (the *qere*, what is *read*).

16. The word *pg'*, sometimes used as "meet," often carries a violent connotation. See Campbell 1975:108.

17. "With this acknowledgment Naomi now includes Ruth in the family . . . Relinquishing isolation, the mother-in-law embraces the daughter-in-law who has already embraced her" (Trible 1978:179).

18. Cf. Berlin (1983:88): "Despite the extensive use of the familial terms 'daughter' and 'daughter-in-law' in connection with Ruth, the narrator keeps reminding us that she is 'the Moabitess'. That she will always bear this label to the natives of Bethlehem is natural—thus the foreman (2:6) and Boaz (4:4, 10) can use it as an objective token of identification. But when the narrator slips it in during private conversations between Ruth and Naomi (2:2, 21) it indicates an underlying tension—an opposition in the story between foreignness and familiality . . . . The story seems to be wrestling with the problem of identity."

19. The great rabbinic scholar Rashi comments: "She said to her: 'Wash yourself and anoint yourself and put on your cloak and afterwards go down to the threshing-floor.' She did not do this, for she said, 'If I go down all dressed up, anyone who meets me and sees me will think I am a harlot.' Therefore she went down in the first place to the threshing-floor and afterwards adorned herself as her mother-in-law had instructed her." (Beattie 1977: 107).

20. For the double entendres of "uncover," "legs/feet," "wing," "lie down/sleep with," "know," "come toward/go into," see Campbell 1975:131-32. "It is simply incomprehensible to me," he writes, " that a Hebrew story-teller could use the words 'uncover,' 'wing,' and a noun for 'legs' which is cognate with a standard euphemism for the sexual organs, all in the same context, and not suggest to his audience that a provocative set of circumstances confronts them" (131). See also the following note 21.

21. The narrator's words "and she came softly (*watabo' balat*)" also allude to another, much more unpleasant, story of entrapment—Jael's entrapment of Sisera: "and she came to him softly (*watabo' 'elayv bala't*) and thrust the tent peg into his mouth [*raqqah*; cf. Songs 4:3, 6:7 where NEB and REB translate "parted lips"]" (Jud 4:21). Campbell (1975:122) notes this parallel as well as 1 Sam 24:4 [Heb 5].

22. See further, above, p. 115 note 28.

23. Perhaps sensing this negative connotation of "the Moabite woman," Berlin leaves this insistent epithet hanging, unexplained: "Ruth is apparently totally accepted when she comes to Bethlehem,

but the narrative continues to refer to her as "the Moabitess" (1988: 263, our italics).

24. As Trible sees it, Ruth's report "hides the extraordinary acts of Ruth and highlights the ordinary acts of Boaz" (1978:186).

25. Reflecting on the fact that Ruth does not tell Naomi of her own initiative at the threshing floor, Trible wonders, "Would a disclosure of what she said be too much for Naomi to bear?" (1978:186). She does not, however, pursue the implications of her question for a reader's reconstruction of Naomi's character. If by the phrase, "too much to bear," a sensitive, fragile character is implied, we would ask, How do such qualities sit with the Naomi who sent Ruth out into the night to uncover Boaz's legs and lie with him? If fragility is the issue, we would suggest that it has to do with Naomi's desperate need for security and self-esteem (here her need to feel in charge) rather than with any sensitivity or pain she might feel on Ruth's behalf.

26. Johanna Bos writes "Whether Boaz actually spoke these words to Ruth or not, obviously Ruth is concerned about Naomi's emptiness" (1988:63).

Berlin (1983:97) recognizes the gap, but takes another stance. In her examination of non-verifiable quoted speech, she categorizes Ruth's speech here as an instance in which "we lack the original speech even though the scene in which it should have occurred is narrated, and the speech is believable." On this text she comments further:

> . . . (I see no reason to view it as a fabrication unless one thinks that Ruth felt obliged to come up with an explanation for the giving of the grain). We can understand it better if we remember that not all direct discourse represents actual speech spoken aloud; some represents thought (or interior monologue). . . .We would then render Ruth's speech as 'He gave me these six measures of barley because he thought that I should not come empty-handed to my mother-in-law.' This is Ruth's perception, psychologically and ideologically, of Boaz's action, made more scenic through quoted direct discourse as she conveys it to Naomi. We don't know why Boaz gave Ruth the barley; we know only why Ruth thought Boaz gave it to her. The absence of the narrator's viewpoint here, which could either confirm or contradict Ruth's is in keeping with the tendency in the Book of Ruth for the narrator to limit his own point of view and have the evaluations made by the characters. (98)

The absence of the narrator's viewpoint is the key here. We don't even know that Ruth thought that Boaz was concerned with Naomi. It makes more sense to understand that Ruth is saying what she thinks Noami wants to hear. She does after all, play upon Naomi's own self-description ("empty"). That Naomi is concerned with emptiness is Ruth's knowledge, not Boaz's.

27. The mention of Rachel, Leah, and Tamar may not, on first reading, seem out of the ordinary in such a blessing. The blessing seems to be dealing with fertility, but only Leah is noted for her fecundity. Rachel was, according to tradition, beautiful and the favorite wife of Jacob, but she was for a long time barren. Perhaps the allusion to Rachel may also be referring to Boaz's attraction to Ruth as well as to Ruth's own lengthy barrenness (cf. Rudolph, cited by Campbell 1975:152). Likewise the allusion to Tamar and the house of Perez points to the foreign woman as an unexpected source of children. Whatever the cause, Tamar was childless and would have remained so if Judah had had his way. A "house of Perez" was never expected. Perhaps the force of the blessing from the people at the gate is the hope for a child where a child may not be expected, in other words, from a woman who was childless from her first marriage.

28. Berlin writes: "Even when the narrator remains within the frame of the story, there are various stances that he may take in relation to it. He may tell the story from an external point of view, as an outside observer looking at a scene or at characters. He would then describe things objectively, seeing what any person present could see" (1983:58).

29. "Cleave" (*dabaq*) is what a man does to a woman when they become "one flesh" (Gen 2:24; 1 Kgs 11:2; cf. Gen 34:3; Josh 23:12). The term "vessels," used of men [*ne'arim*] can be a euphemism for genitalia (1 Sam 21:5[6]). Drinking and eating are often associated with, even symbolic of, love-making (Prov 5:15-19; 9:17; Song of Songs 2:3-5; 4:10-5:1; 7:2,8-9; 8:2). In this context the phrase "go after" may also have a nuance of sexual desire (Prov 7:21-22; Jer 2:23-25). Even the sheaves and the grain can be seen as phallic and semenal images that foreshadow the ultimate gift of "seed" that Boaz will give to Ruth.

30. On "touching" (*ng'*), see above, p. 123 note 12.

31. Pointing to a collocation of motifs and verbal parallels in this chapter, including Boaz's provision for Ruth to draw water from the young men's vessels and the wording of Naomi's blessing in v. 20, Alter has argued that the narrator is making allusion to a "betrothal type scene," especially Genesis 24, the fetching of a wife for Isaac by Abraham's servant (1981:58-60). More accurately, as Hubbard notes (1988:187), the scene is usually a prelude to betrothal, a first meeting which may (by means of the literary convention) portend but not necessarily effect betrothal. Here the scene may signal to a reader a "romantic" outcome but ends with no proposal forthcoming from the male "suitor." Delay leads to reversal: it is the woman, not the man, who makes the next move. Bos calls chapter 3 a "counter-type-scene"

(1988:64). James Williams sees the entire book as countering the traditional "betrothal" type scene (1982:84-85).

32. Bal (1987:71-73), too, has understood Boaz's speech thus.

33. See, for example, Sakenfeld 1985:32-35. Sasson (1979) is an exception.

34. On *kanaph*, see above, p. 114 note 22, and below, pp. 88-90 and p. 128 note 42.

35. On redemption, see below, pp. 88-90; above, p. 114 note 25.

36. Naomi tells Ruth to uncover his *margelot*, a term that occurs only elsewhere in Dan 10:6 where it must mean something like "legs," though the usual term for legs (or feet) would be the word from the same root (*rgl*) *regalim/raglayim* (plural/dual). Perhaps Naomi uses a more discrete word to avoid saying directly "uncover his legs," though that is what she appears to have in mind, especially given the use of *regel* as a euphemism for genitals. See Campbell 1975:131.

37. This point is made well by Phillips 1986:13-14. We came across this article too late to incorporate comment in the body of our book. With some significant parts of his argument we are in disagreement, especially (a) his claim that there is an unstated requirement that Boaz really should offer levirate marriage (what is the evidence? why does that requirement not apply to the nearer redeemer?); (b) his assertion that Ruth's foreignness is no problem; (c) his understanding that Naomi is only interested in raising up Elimelech's name; (d) his insistence on reading the *qere*. The strength of his argument as we see it is the recognition of Boaz's susceptibility to the pressures of reputation—"For the sudden marriage of the rich Boaz with the foreign widow could only result in widespread comment and provoke malicious gossip" (15).

38. Cf. Phillips: "By making the redemption of land appear to be the legal issue before the court, Boaz found a way of securing his reputation" (1986:15). Phillips's discussion of the way Boaz makes himself look good by contrast with the near redeemer is quite close to ours except that he understands the issues somewhat differently.

39. Watson (1908:398) asks the same question. See also Hubbard 1988:204-205.

40. A difficulty remains. If Ruth's Moabiteness is the fundamental bar to marriage between her and Boaz, what are we to make of Boaz's assertion, at the end of his response on the threshing floor, that "all the gate of my people knows that you are a woman of worth (*'eshet hayil*)" (3:11). The feminine term, *'eshet hayil*, is, of course, as slippery as its masculine counterpart, *'ish gibbôr hayil*. Whether Boaz actually means to say that she is a woman of worth or whether he means to describe her as something like "a woman of character" or "a woman of determination" is unclear. The phrase, like many others in this story, *does* more than it *says*. What he intends, what she hears, and

the nuances recognized by the reader make for many possible levels of meaning.

Furthermore, the immediate context gives the description an additional twist. "Fear not" clauses commonly reassure by asserting that what is perceived to be a problem is not really a problem, that what seems to be in doubt is not really in doubt. ("You shall speak," says YHWH to Jeremiah; "Fear them not, for I am with you to deliver you" [cf. Jer 1:7-8]. "Fear not," says God to Isaac, "for I am with you, and I will bless you and multiply your descendants . . . ." [Gen 26:24]. "Fear not," says the midwife to Rachel, "for now you will have another son" [Gen 35:17].) The present expression, therefore, reinforces our view that what is at stake in the present situation, certainly as far as Boaz understands it, is a matter of communally perceived "worth." His somewhat premature reassurance, therefore, must be understood as a half-truth. He is offering comfort and hope (playing the part of God again!). Tact prevents him from stating outright the facts of the matter. Rather, he discreetly shifts back into the present what he hopes to achieve on the morrow. With luck, marriage to the "man of worth" will see "worth" rubbing off on the wife; perhaps, then, as the Moabite woman gives way to the wife of Boaz, her own worth may even be permitted to show.

In aid of the half-truth is that odd expression, "all the gate of my people." Indeed the whole gate (literally speaking) knows of Ruth's worth (and certainly her "character" and "determination"). It has witnessed her arrival with her mother-in-law, seen her go out into the fields, and down to the threshing floor. If, as seems likely, the expression is idiomatic for either the assembly at the gate (see Campbell 1975:124 note 11), or simply, more generally, it is metonymic for the essential city, its choice here in place of a direct expression of "people" is apt, for it allows Boaz the licence he needs.

41. Phillips is one exception—he does try to deal with precisely this question. On Boaz as trickster, see Sasson 1979:230-31.

42. The phrase "spread your *kanaph*" is often taken as an explicit invitation to marriage (cf. Hubbard 1988:212). Though that meaning would keep things nicely above board in this scene the phrase cannot so simply be determined.

The spreading of a *kanaph* read as "wing" has a protective connotation as in, e.g., Deut 32:11, a connotation that echoes Boaz's reference to YHWH's wings being a source of refuge. The spreading of a *kanaph* read as "skirt" occurs elsewhere only in Ezek 16:8 in a metaphor describing YHWH's relationship to Israel: "And I passed by you and I saw you and behold your time was a time for love [or lovers]. I spread my skirt over you and I covered your nakedness. I swore to you and I entered into covenant with you, says the lord YHWH, and you became mine." Many commentators are eager to understand the spreading of the skirt here as an act of betrothal. The significance of spreading the skirt, however, is not so clear. The terms "swearing" and "entering into covenant" are very general; the verb "to betroth" (*'eres*) is not used. If, however, YHWH's oath and covenant denote betrothal, the spreading of the skirt chronologically precedes the oath and the contract and, in fact, takes place in a sexually suggestive situation. (It is not surprising that a mind as provocatively lewd as that of Ezekiel could portray YHWH's desire for Israel in such lusty terms.) It is interesting to note in connection with the Ruth text that, once Boaz agrees to do all that Ruth has asked, i.e., to spread his *kanaph*, he does a little "swearing" of his own (v. 13).

43. Here we differ significantly from many commentators (most recently, Hubbard 1988:48-52) who assume that when Ruth calls Boaz a *go'el* she implies that he is reponsible for redeeming her (or Naomi's) property and, by extension, is obligated to offer her levirate marriage. This assumption is usually bolstered by another, namely that the phrase *parash kanaph* ("spread a skirt") is used when offering or requesting marriage (see above, p. 128 note 42). Despite the assurance with which commentators make these claims, there is a long history of exegetical dispute over the issues.

44. In 2:20 Naomi has mentioned to her that Boaz is a relative (*qarov lanu*), "one of our redeemers" (*miggo'alenu hu'*); but Naomi noticeably fails to use the term "*go'el*" in prefacing the trip to the threshing floor. This feature of the text obviously suggests to the reader that she does not expect this particular institution to be a matter of special concern for either Ruth or Boaz on this occasion.

45. Commentators who assert otherwise are usually trying to explain the present text. Consequently this text has given rise to frequent exercises in circular argument.

46. Although in 4:3 Boaz speaks to the near-redeemer ("Mr. So and So") about "our brother Elimelech," the usage here is general, meaning something like "kinsman." If Boaz were a real brother of Elimelech, it is inconceivable that neither the narrator nor Naomi call him "brother" when speaking of him (2:1; 2:20 and 3:2), but instead use broader terms meaning "kinsman." Moreover, in the levirate law, the 'brothers" who are involved in a levirate responsibility are defined as "brothers who dwell together," a condition which does not fit Boaz, even if he were a real brother.

47. Many English translations use the word "buy" (NEB and NASB are exceptions), but nowhere else in the Hebrew Bible is *qanah* used of marriage. (Appeal to Mishnaic usage [e.g., Weiss 1964:244-48] is a retrospective fallacy.) Besides, from whom would Boaz be buying her? Naomi? That seems improbable. Likewise, commentators who talk of Ruth as a chattel of the estate can cite no clear biblical evidence for their view. "Acquire" is the better choice, easily applying both to the field and to Ruth (against Hubbard 1988:240, 243-44 who asserts categorically that the word here means "buy" or "purchase" but then

defines purchase as meaning "to marry as part of a legally valid transaction," so that Ruth is not literally "bought"). It is easy to understand Boaz deliberately sliding from the commercial meaning "buy" in regard to the field to the general meaning "acquire" in regard to Ruth, while retaining (in Hebrew) a symmetry between the two proposed courses of action.

48. A slight emendation of the verse is required, whether one follows the vocalized text (*qere*) or consonantal text (*kethib*). The word *ûme'et* (literally, "and from [with]") has long been recognized as a scribal error for *gam 'et-* ("also [+ the sign of the definite object]") which is what appears later, in v. 10). As the verse stands it leaves the verb "I [or you] acquire" without an object.

49. We wonder about the cash value of the land. After all, if the widows are indeed destitute, why has Naomi not sold it herself? Why has no one been interested in it previously? Can it be that the land, for whatever reason, is not a very desirable piece of property for redemption? On the land and sale, see also above, p. 118 note 47.

50. The problems with following the *qere* abound. Among them is the simple question, If redemption of the field brought with it an obligation to marry, as the *qere* implies, how was it that the redeemer, who clearly knew about the rules of redemption, knew nothing of this drastic requirement, or, alternatively (Hubbard 1988:61), knew of Naomi but not of Ruth? The answer is far from apparent. But that is only the beginning. There is no evidence that a woman in ancient Israel could be entailed with a field for purposes of marriage, and all attempts at basing the legalities concerned on some postulated *ge'ullah* marriage, marriage tied to redemption, are extremely tenuous (for a recent attempt, see Hubbard 1988:48-62). To read the *kethib* is to take a much simpler road. On the problems with the *qere*, see Sasson 1978a, 1978b, 1979:122-136; Beattie 1971, 1974, 1978a, 1978b.

51. Thus Beattie (see above, note 50) rightly argues that Boaz's announcement at the city gate concerns a simple case of the remarriage of a widow. But in attempting to rid the text of levirate marriage altogether Beattie misses the point of Boaz deliberately using the language of levirate marriage: "to restore the name of the dead to his inheritance" (v. 5) and "to perpetuate the name of the dead in his inheritance that the name of the dead be not cut off from among his brothers and from the gate of his place" (v. 10). Moreover, the narrator cements this understanding for the reader by dwelling on the shoe ceremony, thereby alluding unmistakably to Deut 25:5-10.

52. Indeed, according to Rashi (who is reading the *kethib*), the near redeemer refuses to continue with the transaction because he believes (mistakenly, Rashi thinks) that to marry a Moabite woman would be to destroy his inheritance, assuming the law against a Moabite entering the assembly (Deut 23:4). See Beattie 1977:109.

53. Many critics have claimed, with reason, that levirate marriage (here and in general) was designed to take care of the widow as well as raise up the name of the dead man. See, e.g., Campbell 1975:136, on Ruth, and Davies 1981:142-44, on the custom in general, though Davies admits that issues of property and male line were primary. The primary concern of the custom, however, must have largely been a matter of point of view. To women, the custom would have been important because it offered them some semblance of security. To men, the custom promised a kind of generational immortality—the preservation of male name and property throughout the generations.

What is noticeable in Ruth 4 is that Boaz, in speaking to the body of male elders, appeals to male interests. He does not propose meeting the subsistence needs of impoverished widows; rather, he focuses on the incorporeal male values—the sacred male name and lineage. As Trible puts it, "Boaz presents the situation of these women quite differently from their own understanding of it. He subordinates both of them to male prerogatives; the buying of land and the restoration of the name of the dead to his inheritance. . . . [I]n a private conversation with Ruth, Boaz made her welfare the sole object of his concern, but in a public discussion with men he makes Ruth the means for achieving a male purpose"(1978:192). Cf. Bos (1986:36-37): "it must be admitted that the repeated interest in vss. 1-12 is directed more toward the dead males in Naomi's family, and to Boaz himself, than to Ruth and Naomi."

54. Thus, for example, Goslinga (1986:517):

Its overall design and, especially, its conclusion show that its aim was to make known the history of David's ancestors. It discloses the genealogical line by which God's favorite king was descended from the patriarch Judah and, no less, the true piety and nobility that were the marks of his forebears. Since the book's main character is a Moabite who is presented in a very favorable light, we can also discern another purpose. It reveals how even heathendom played a role in the formation of the royal house chosen by God and how this did not put a blemish on David's family, since Ruth, his great grandmother, wholeheartedly accepted the God of Israel and gladly became a member of His chosen people.

Clearly, this understanding of the story's purpose is especially popular among scholars who date the book of Ruth during the period of Ezra and Nehemiah, viewing it as a polemic against nationalistic religious reforms.

55. The commentaries are replete with such moves. Thus Hubbard sees as a main theme "eclips[ing] all others" in the book the fact that "the triumph of Elimelech's family over tragedy gave Israel King David." The child born was "ordained for some great destiny." "Once

Boaz had the rights to Ruth, the author began to point to the story's larger, more important outcome . . . God's preservation of Elimelech's worthy family line resulted in the advent of King David. It is the event at which the story's implicit sense of great destiny aimed . . . Of course, this outcome vindicated Naomi's patient suffering: she became the honored ancestress of that leading family (4:15, 17b)" (Hubbard 1988:65). Not Ruth's family but Elimelech's. Of Ruth, no mention in all this, except as the convenient object of a man's "rights." She and her child are but channels for "the advent of King David." The terms that measure the worth of both mother and child are simple—their capacity to produce someone else's genes. And in the final irony of this reading, even Ruth's function as birth canal is usurped, by "patient" Naomi, who offers King David no genes at all! When Ruth is finally given her due (p. 66) it is in familiar terms. Her ultimate reward "was Israel's admiration of [her] as David's ancestor."

56. Cf. Trible's comment about Ruth and Orpah's *hesed*: "[T]he past loyalty of human beings (foreign women, at that) is a paradigm for the future kindness of the divine human being" (1978:170). Campbell includes Boaz in this God paradigm: "We can say that persons act as God to one another in our story. If that be so, how striking it is that Ruth falls on her face and bows to the earth—worship language in most instances in the OT—before Boaz, and responds to his blessing of her in YHWH's name by calling him "my lord" (1975:113).

57. Jewish tradition records the racial prejudice likely to meet the Moabite women in Bethlehem: "[Naomi's] two daughters-in-law were very dear to her on account of the love they had borne her sons . . . Yet she would not take them with her to Palestine, for she saw contemptuous treatment in store for them as Moabitish women" (Ginzberg 1913:31, citing Zohar Ruth). Several of our students have urged this reading. In particular, Steve Singleton, Eddie Adams, and Ruth Espinoza have helped us see its substance by offering illuminating analogies from their own racial and cultural experiences.

The same passage in Zohar Ruth talks of a further problem that would confront the young women, namely class prejudice. We, too, see class as a social barrier between the important landowner Boaz and the impoverished foreigner, Ruth.

58. Trible, missing the gender distinction, claims that Ruth 's comment here is an assurance that "she can provide for the two of them" and that she "is not looking for a husband" (1978:180).

59. This absence of Naomi from Boaz's speech forms a major obstacle for commentators who want to find Naomi as a significant object of Boaz's concern. Hubbard even has Boaz "willing to sacrifice his own means, his own life for two impoverished widows" (1988:73).

60. The phrase "to speak to the heart" appears to be a perlocutionary expression, that is, one describing a speech act which produces consequential effects on the feelings, thoughts or actions of its hearer

—in other words, a successfully completed action, like the verbs "convince" or "compel" in English as distinct from "urge" or "advise." In both Gen 50:21 and Ruth 2:13 the phrase is paired with the verb "to comfort" (*niham*). Hence the RSV translation of Gen 50:21, "Thus he reassured them (*wayenahem*)." On the other hand, like many versions, the RSV translation of 3:13, "for you have . . . spoken kindly to your maidservant," is too weak and misses the perlocutionary sense. On perlocutionary language, see Austin 1962:99-103.

61. "In essence, Ruth asked Boaz to answer his own prayer!" (Hubbard 1988:212; cf. also Trible 1978:184).

62. Trible has rightly pointed us to the ambiguous nature of Ruth's obedience to Naomi: "[Ruth's] reply differs from her earlier responses to the topic of a husband. In scene one Ruth's allegiance to Naomi superseded that need; in scene two Ruth's struggle for their physical survival submerged that need; here in scene three Ruth's allegiance to Naomi accords with that need. *Loyalty to self* and to mother-in-law signifies for Ruth a movement from dissent to perseverance to consent" (1978:182; our italics).

63. Some of our contemplation of this "ending" we discover also in the thoughts and feelings of Hartsoe's Ruth, in the beginning and ending of her letter to Orpah (1981:30, 34):

> I sit looking out at the fields of grain and watching the reapers at work. My husband Boaz is wealthy and I do not have to help in the harvest. In fact, I do not have much of anything to do. Even my little boy is being cared for by Naomi. I am lonely, Orpah, and I have no one with whom to share my feelings. Often I wonder how things have gone for you . . . Naomi took my child and treated him as if she were the mother. The other women even called him "Naomi's son." His name, Obed, was given him by the family. Even today it is still as if I had no part in his birth. I wonder if years from now when family histories are being sung, will the singer say "son of Naomi" or "son of Ruth," or will both of us be forgotten and only the words "son of Boaz" endure?
>
> I am still your sister-in-law,
>
> Ruth

BIBLIOGRAPHY

Alter, Robert. 1981. *The Art of Biblical Narrative*. New York: Basic Books.

Auld, A. Graeme. 1984. *Joshua, Judges, and Ruth*. The Daily Study Bible Series. Philadelphia: Westminster.

Austin, J. L. 1967. *How to do Things with Words*. Oxford: Oxford Univ.

Bal, Mieke. 1985. *Narratology: Introduction to the Theory of Narrative*. Transl. by Christine van Boheemen. Toronto: Univ. of Toronto.

—— 1987. *Lethal Love: Literary Readings of Biblical Love Stories*. Indiana Studies in Biblical Literature. Bloomington, IN: Indiana Univ.

—— 1988. "Tricky Thematics." In J. Cheryl Exum and Johanna W. H. Bos, eds., *Reasoning with the Foxes: Female Wit in a World of Male Power*. [*Semeia* 42]. Atlanta: Scholars. Pp. 133-155.

Bankson, Marjory Zoet. 1987. *Seasons of Friendship: Naomi and Ruth as a Pattern*. San Diego, CA: LuraMedia.

Bar-Efrat, Shimon. 1989. *Narrative Art in the Bible*. Dorothea Shefer-Vanson, trans. Bible & Literature Series. Sheffield, UK: Almond.

Beattie, D.R.G. 1971. "Kethibh and Qere in Ruth 4:5." *VT* 21:490-94.

—— 1974. "The Book of Ruth as Evidence of Israeltie Legal Practice." *VT* 24:251-67.

—— 1977. *Jewish Exegesis of the Book of Ruth*. JSOT Supplements. Sheffield, UK: JSOT.

—— 1978a. "Ruth III." *JSOT* 5:39-48.

—— 1978b. "Redemption in Ruth, and Related Matters: A Response to Jack M. Sasson." *JSOT* 5:65-68.

Berlin, Adele. 1983. *Poetics and Interpretation of Biblical Narrative*. Bible and Literature Series. Sheffield, UK: Almond.

—— 1988. "Ruth." *Harpers Bible Commentary*. James L. Mays, ed. San Francisco: Harper & Row. Pp. 262-267.

Bos, Johanna W. H. 1986. *Ruth, Esther, Jonah*. Knox Preaching Guides. Atlanta: John Knox.

—— 1988. "Out of the Shadows: Genesis 38; Judges 4:17-22; Ruth 3." *Semeia* 42:37-67.

Campbell, Edward F., Jr. 1975. *Ruth: A New Translation with Introduction and Commentary*. Garden City: Doubleday.

Campbell, Edward F., and Paul J. Achtemeier. 1987. "The Book of Ruth." In *Harpers Bible Dictionary*. San Francisco: Harper & Row. P. 876.

Chatman, Seymour. 1978. *Story and Discourse: Narratiave Structure in Fiction and Film.* Ithaca & London: Cornell Univ.

Davies, E. W. 1981. "Inheritance Rights and the Hebrew Levirate Marriage." *VT* 31:138-44 [Part I], 257-68 [Part 2].

Duffy, Maureen. 1985. "Mother and the Girl." *Collected Poems 1949-1984.* Hamish Hamilton. Pp. 282-84.

Fewell, Danna Nolan. 1987. "Feminist Reading of the Hebrew Bible: Affirmation, Resistance and Transformation." *JSOT* 39:77-87.

Fewell, Danna Nolan and David M. Gunn. 1991 (forthcoming). "Tipping the Balance: Sternberg's Reader and the Rape of Dinah," *Journal of Biblical Literature.*

Ginzberg, Louis. 1913. *The Legends of the Jews.* Vol. IV. Philadelphia: Jewish Publication Society.

Goslinga, C. J. 1986. *Joshua, Judges, Ruth.* Bible Student's Commentary. Grand Rapids, MI: Regency/Zondervan.

Gray, John. 1967. *Joshua, Judges and Ruth.* New Century Bible.

Green, Barbara. 1982. "The Plot of the Biblical Story of Ruth." *JSOT* 23:55-68.

Gunkel, Hermann. 1928. *What Remains of the Old Testament, and Other Essays.* A. K. Dallas, trans. New York: Macmillan.

Gunn, David M. 1990. "Reading Right: Reliable and Omniscient Narrator, Omniscient God, and Foolproof Composition in the Hebrew Bible." In *The Bible in Three Dimensions,* David J. A. Clines, Stephen E. Fowl, Stanley E. Porter, eds. JSOT Supplements. Sheffield, UK: JSOT.

Gunn, David M. and Danna Nolan Fewell. 1991. *Old Testament Narrative.* Oxford Bible Series. London & New York: Oxford Univ.

Hals, Ronald. 1969. *The Theology of the Book of Ruth.* Facet Books; Philadelphia: Fortress.

Hartsoe, Colleen Ivey. 1981. *Dear Daughter: Letters from Eve and Other Women of the Bible.* Wilton, CT: Morehouse-Barlow.

Holbert, John. 1991 (forthcoming). *Reading and Preaching the Hebrew Bible: A Narrative Approach.* Nashville: Abingdon.

Hopkins, David C.. 1985. *The Highlands of Canaan: Agricultural Life in the Early Iron Age.* The Social World of Biblical Antiquity Series. Sheffield, UK: Almond.

Hubbard, Robert L., Jr. 1988. *The Book of Ruth.* New International Commentary on the Old Testament; Grand Rapids: Eerdmans.

Joüon, Paul. 1953. *Ruth: commentaire philologique et exégétique.* Rome: Institut Biblique Pontifical.

Levine, Étan. 1973. *The Aramaic Version of Ruth.* Analecta Biblica. Rome: Pontifical Biblical Institute.

Manning, Samuel. 1890. *'Those Holy Fields': Palestine. Illustrated by Pen and Pencil.* London: The Religious Tract Society.

Marshall, Effie Lawrence. 1949. *The World's Most Famous Love Story.* Portland, Maine: Falmouth Publishing.

Niditch, Susan. 1979. "The Wronged Woman Righted: An Analysis of Genesis 38." *Harvard Theological Review* 72:143-49.

Patrick, Dale. 1981. *The Rendering of God in the Old Testament.* Overtures to Biblical Theology. Philadelphia: Fortress.

Phelan, James. 1989. *Reading People, Reading Plots: Character, Progression, and the Interpretation of Narrative.* Chicago & London: Univ. of Chicago.

Phillips, Anthony. 1986. "The Book of Ruth—Deception and Shame." *Journal of Jewish Studies* 37:1-17.

Preminger, Alex, and Edward L. Greenstein, eds. 1986. *The Hebrew Bible in Literary Criticism.* New York: Ungar Publishing.

Sakenfeld, Katharine Doob. 1985. *Faithfulness in Action: Loyalty in Biblical Perspective.* Overtures to Biblical Theology. Philadelphia: Fortress.

Sasson, Jack M. 1978a. "Ruth III: A Response." *JSOT* 5:49-51.

—— 1978b. "The Issue of *Ge'ullah* in Ruth." *JSOT* 5:52-64.

—— 1979. *Ruth: A New Translation with a Philological Commentary and a Formalist-Folklorist Interpretation.* Baltimore & London: Johns Hopkins Univ.

Spence, H. E.. 1924. *Ruth: A Dramatization in Biblical History.* Nashville: Cokesbury.

Sternberg, Meir. 1985. *The Poetics of Biblical Narrative: Ideological Literature and the Drama of Reading.* Indiana Literary Biblical Series. Bloomington, IN: Indiana Univ.

Trible, Phyllis. 1978. "A Human Comedy." *God and the Rhetoric of Sexuality.* Philadelphia: Fortress. 166-99.

Watson, Robert A. 1908. *Judges and Ruth.* Expositors Bible. London: Hodder & Stoughton.

Weiss, David. 1964. "The Use of QNH in Connection with Marriage." *Harvard Theological Review* 57:2243-58.

Williams, James G. 1982. *Women Recounted: Narrative Thinking and the God of Israel.* Sheffield, UK: Almond.

Wojcik, Jan. 1985. "Improvising Rules in the Book of Ruth." *Publications of the Modern Language Association of America* 100:145-153.

JSOT = *Journal for the Study of the Old Testament*
VT = *Vetus Testamentum*

INDEXES

AUTHORS

NAMES AND SUBJECTS

BIBLICAL REFERENCES

JPS TANAKH = Jewish Publication Society Tanakh
KJV = King James Version
NASB = New American Standard Bible
NEB = New English Bible
REB = Revised English Bible
RSV = Revised Standard Version

LXX = Septuagint
MT = Masoretic Text